Crimes, Courts and Figures
An Introduction to Criminal Statistics

Nigel Walker

Penguin Books

Penguin Books Ltd, Harmondsworth,
Middlesex, England
Penguin Books Inc., 7110 Ambassador Road,
Baltimore, Md 21207, U.S.A.
Penguin Books Australia Ltd,
Ringwood, Victoria, Australia

First published 1971
Copyright © Nigel Walker, 1971

Made and printed in Great Britain by
Cox & Wyman Ltd, London, Reading and Fakenham
Set in Monotype Times

Contents

Editorial Foreword

Previous volumes in this series have examined the impact of law upon the social problems of road accidents and racial discrimination in employment, and have described the relationship of law with the machinery of local government. This book is very different. It offers an account of techniques necessary to a functional appreciation of the criminal law; how to understand and (as important) how not to misunderstand the statistics which register the results of what the criminal law does.

The study of law has perhaps been less illuminated by statistical analysis than any other social science. Most lawyers, however articulate and literate, are not trained to use elementary tools of quantitative analysis. Yet in the discussion about 'trends' of the incidence of crimes, or about the deterrent effect of various types of punishment, or of the 'normal range' of criminal sentences, and the many similar phrases into which lawyers and others are led in current discussions of 'law and order', these tools are essential requirements for avoidance of judgment by 'hunch', in other words of the numerical equivalent of illiteracy. Law students spend many hours with *mens rea*. Yet how many of them can be confident when asked about the likelihood of 'sampling errors' in a survey of sentenced offenders, or even about the usage of such terms as 'mode', 'mean' and 'median'?

For the lawyer then, this book offers an introduction to ways of thinking which allow him to assess more readily the effects of the criminal law in society and the reliability of his own views about its efficacy. Criminology has led the way in opening up the workings of the legal process to such scientific study; and the author leads the reader gently through what are often thought to be complexities, amply fulfilling his promise that he demands no more than 'elementary arithmetic' and 'common sense'.

To students of other social sciences who may be better acquainted with statistics than the lawyer, this volume affords an example of such techniques applied to crime, to the criminal and to punishment. To them the problem of the 'unreported offence', the difficulty of assessing 'causality' or of discovering 'mis-classification' may perhaps have a more familiar ring; and they will find a concise and original account of such problems in the interpretation of criminal statistics.

The law lives not merely in rules inscribed in statutes or in principles drawn from judicial decisions, but in its effects upon and application to human beings. To understand the law about theft, we need to know not merely the relevant rules of law but how often thieves are known, apprehended or 'cautioned' but not prosecuted; and what happens to those who are convicted and sentenced by different courts or to those who do and do not appeal. For such an understanding we sorely need a helping hand with the interpretation of elementary statistics. It was, therefore, with joy that we, as lawyers, welcomed into this series the text which follows, written by one of the most distinguished scholars in British criminology.

O.K.F.
K.W.W.

Preface

This book is written for the non-statistician who needs to make use of criminal statistics. It is not, however, an attempt to turn him into a statistician. Instead, it tries to show how much is possible in the way of interpretation without any sophisticated techniques. All it demands of the reader are two things. One is elementary arithmetic, up to the level of the calculation of percentages – and even this can be done by using the simplest form of slide-rule. The other is the sort of common sense which can see behind the figures to the real events which they summarize. An example of what happens when one fails to do so can be found in Ernest Hooton's monumental study of 4212 adult male white inmates of American penitentiaries, which reported the finding that 'first degree murderers showed an excess of widowers'. If he had asked who their victims had been he might have found this less noteworthy.[1]

Although this book is not an attack on social statisticians, it is an attempt to remedy two omissions of which they are often guilty. One is a neglect of what may be called the 'grass-roots' of their subject, by which I mean the situations in which events involving human beings are converted into numbers by other fallible human beings. I hope to show how important the grass-roots are to the proper use of criminal statistics (and, I suspect, of any other sort of social statistics, although I know of no books which do the same for them). The other omission is the result of preoccupation with technique. Most users of social statistics need them to answer fairly simple questions by the simplest means; but the textbooks are intent on the sophisticated techniques which are needed by research workers. One of the aims of this book is to demonstrate what one can get out of criminal statistics without such techniques.

1. See *The American Criminal: An Anthropological Study*, vol. 1, Harvard University Press, 1939, p. 259.

Finally the chief effect which books on social statistics have on many readers is to increase their scepticism about the possibility of basing any reliable inference on figures. Hence the cliché 'You can prove anything with statistics.' It would be nearer the truth to say that you can *dis*prove *some* things with them; but in fact the truth is even less discouraging than that. Provided that one knows how the figures were compiled, and provided that one is able to use the sort of common sense which I have mentioned, plus a few rules which I shall explain, a number of interesting and useful inferences about crime and our penal system can be safely made. One aim of this book is to show that this can be done often enough to justify the study of criminal statistics by non-statisticians.

This book owes a great deal to comments, criticisms and suggestions made by the following friends who were kind enough to read the first draft: Mr N. C. Abbott, Pembroke College, Oxford, Mr A. J. Ashworth, New College, Oxford, Mr R. A. Carr-Hill and Mr K. Hope, Nuffield College, Oxford, Mrs E. Gibson and Mr R. T. Tudor of the Home Office's Statistical Division, Mrs S. F. McCabe of the Oxford Penal Research Unit, and Mr D. J. Steer, St Catherine's College, Oxford. Thanks are also due to Mr F. H. McClintock and Mr N. H. Avison for allowing me to incorporate tables from *Crimes of Violence* and *Crime in England and Wales*; to Mr L. T. Wilkins and Tavistock Publications for allowing me to use material from *Social Deviance*; to the Edinburgh University Press for allowing me to incorporate a section from my textbook *Crime and Punishment in Britain*, and to Allen Lane The Penguin Press for allowing me to incorporate a section from my book *Sentencing in a Rational Society*; and to Her Majesty's Stationery Office for permission to reproduce tables from the *Criminal Statistics, England and Wales* and an extract from the report of the Perks Committee.

Introduction

Some people like numbers for their own sake, either because they are mathematically inclined, or because numerals give them a feeling of certainty and tidiness which is lacking in real life. Unless one is a mathematician, however, the rational use of numbers is as a basis for inferences and decisions. Criminal statistics, like other social statistics, occasionally provide some problems for mathematicians[1]; but for the most part they are of more interest to lawyers, police, probation officers, legislators and administrators, who need them in order to answer practical questions. Is violent crime increasing in frequency or seriousness? If traced, how likely is an offender to be convicted or acquitted by a jury, or by a bench of magistrates? If convicted what is his sentence likely to be? Are sentencers becoming more or less severe? What is the effect of introducing a new measure, such as the suspended prison sentence? How effective are sentences as deterrents or correctives? How long are typical prison sentences? Can one distinguish between offenders who will keep out of trouble in future from those who will not? If so, in what circumstances is it practicable (and justifiable) to do so?

These are examples of questions which used to be, and sometimes still are, answered by impression and hunch, but which ought not to be answered without statistical information. This book discusses the ways in which they have been or might be answered, and the fallacies which have to be avoided in doing so.

'Statistics' is an ambiguous word. It can mean 'the technique of basing inferences on figures', and in this sense requires some degree of mathematical skill; or it can simply mean 'the figures' themselves. This is what it means in the title of this book, which – as the Preface

1. See, for example, R. A. Carr-Hill's article in *The Violent Offender – Reality or Illusion?* (1970) and M. A. P. Willmer's *Crime and Information Theory* (1970).

indicates – is concerned not with mathematical techniques but with what can be inferred from figures about crime without technical expertise. Even so, the term 'criminal statistics' is usually employed rather loosely to include not only information about reported breaches of the criminal law (that is, criminal statistics in the strict sense) but also numbers of persons tried and sentenced (more precisely known as 'criminal judicial statistics') as well as figures for sentenced offenders who are, say, on probation or in prison. This last category is sometimes called 'penal statistics' or, in the case of prisons and similar establishments, 'custodial statistics'. All three kinds, and several others, are discussed in the first seven chapters of this book, in a more-or-less logical sequence from the reporting – or non-reporting – of a crime to the reception of offenders into prison and their subsequent reconviction.

Like other social statistics, however, all these subdivisions of criminal statistics must be broadly distinguished into two kinds: 'routinely collected' and 'specially collected'. The published annual *Criminal Statistics, England and Wales* (which the reader will need to have by him if he is to get the maximum benefit from this book) is an example of routinely collected statistics, being based on forms compiled by police forces and sent at regular intervals to the Home Office's Statistical Division, where they are processed by a computer. Other examples will be found in Appendix B of this book.

Often, however, as we shall see, routine statistics cannot answer important questions, or at least cannot do so with sufficient reliability or precision. Special investigations have to be launched in order to collect representative samples of whatever type of event or person is the subject of the question. Sometimes these samples are simply taken from routinely collected information: for instance, from the Home Office's card-index of persons convicted of 'standard list offences' (see the Glossary of Technical Terms, page 137). Sometimes the investigators have to sample at the grass-roots. Examples of specially collected statistics will be found in McClintock's *Crimes of Violence* (1963) or in Ennis's (1967) report of the survey of potential victims which is described here in Chapter 1.

A good deal of this book is devoted to the interpretation of routine criminal and judicial statistics. There is at least one sort of event, however, which is of great importance from the point of view both of

12 Introduction

criminology and of law enforcement, but which routine statistics, collected by official agencies such as the police, cannot be expected to record, and which can be studied only through specially collected statistics. This is the unreported offence, which is discussed in the first chapter.

Chapter 1
Unreported Offences

The problem of the 'dark figure' – the unrecorded percentage of the events which one is trying to study – is common to all the social sciences. Social psychiatrists, for example, would dearly like to have sound estimates of the numbers of people in the population who are suffering from undiagnosed mental disorders; and attempts have been made to arrive at such estimates by using general practitioners as reporting agents. In criminology the dark figure of unrecorded crime is of interest not only to the sociologist but also to the penologist who wants, for example, to assess the deterrent or corrective efficacy of penal measures.

Why Unreported?

An offence may be unrecorded although it is reported to the police, as we shall see later. For the moment, however, we are concerned with the offence which does not reach the ears of the police. This can happen for a large number of reasons, each of which is worth brief consideration.

1. The persons involved, whether as participants or witnesses, may simply fail to realize that an offence is being committed. Many children and even adolescents commit criminal assaults and indecencies upon each other without being aware that they are breaking the law. A motorist can infringe many prohibitions without realizing it. His silencer, his brakes, his lights, his windscreen-wiper may be criminally defective; he may be exceeding the speed-limit without realizing it; and so on.

2. Those involved may know that an offence has been committed, but have been willing parties to it. This is often the case with homosexual

offences, illegal abortions and contraventions of traffic regulations. Even people who happen to know that an offence has been committed but are not personally concerned may see no harm in it, or even approve, either because they disagree with the law or because they dislike the victim: poaching provides frequent examples of this.

3. The offender may know that he has committed an offence, but the victim may not. A child sometimes does not realize that what an adult has done to him or her is criminal. The owner of a business may not know that he is the victim of pilfering or embezzlement by one of his employees.

4. There may be no 'victim' in the usual sense of the word. Who is the victim when litter is dropped in a public place? Or when a man lies 'drunk and incapable' in a public square? Offences of this kind come to official notice usually as a result of being observed by the police rather than reported by the public, and the police are often selective in taking notice of them – a problem which will be discussed later.

5. Even when there is a personal victim who knows that an offence has been committed against him against his will, it is by no means always reported. The victim may be restrained from going to the police for a wide variety of reasons. He may be too frightened of the offender's retaliation; an American survey, which will be mentioned later, found that this was the main reason for non-reporting of a substantial number of assaults. He may himself have been behaving criminally, and even if not he may be antagonistic to the police. He may think that they will be quite unable to trace the offender (as indeed they are in the case of many petty thefts). He may think that the consequences of reporting it will have too drastic an effect on the offender: employers who detect employees in pilfering not infrequently dismiss them instead of reporting them to the police. Sometimes, too, the victim wants to remain on good terms with the offender: some employers connive at pilfering for this reason. The victim may be too embarrassed to report the offence: this is often the case when a woman has been sexually assaulted, especially if she feels that her own conduct may be questioned. Finally, the American survey just mentioned found that some victims were 'too confused, or did not know how to report'.

16   Unreported Offences

Why Unrecorded?

A wholly different set of reasons may dissuade the police from taking official notice of an offence even when this is committed in their presence. Their reasoning is usually economic, in the widest sense of the word. To issue a summons against every person whom they see dropping litter, driving at a few miles an hour above the speed-limit, fighting in a school playground, using words likely to provoke a breach of the peace at a demonstration, would often be impossible, and usually a wasteful use of manpower that is better employed in other ways. Another consideration is their relations with the public; too many prosecutions for trivial offences might alienate citizens on whom police can normally rely for help.

Even when a citizen reports an offence and is prepared to give evidence, the police sometimes prefer not to take official notice. This seems to be particularly frequent in the case of minor domestic violence. A wife who arrives at a police station to complain of being knocked about by her husband will usually be told that she can 'lay an information' before the magistrates herself, but that the police will not. The reason is sometimes said to be that section 42 of the Offences against the Person Act 1861 provides only for proceedings to be initiated by the complaint of the aggrieved person; and that unless actual bodily harm has been done the police cannot act. This is not so, however: section 47 of the same act, though it deals mainly with assault which occasions bodily harm, also allows them to act where the assault does not, although they rarely do so. The real reason is probably a feeling that trivial quarrels, especially domestic ones, are best left to simmer down without official intervention, together with the well-founded fear that if prosecution is initiated the complainant will quickly decide that he or she does not really want to see the offender in the dock after all. The number of prosecutions for common assault in which the charge is withdrawn, or dismissed for want of the necessary evidence, runs into thousands each year.

Estimating the Dark Figure

Accurate estimates of the volume of unreported crime are, for obvious reasons, impossible. Investigations[1] which involve asking samples of

1. Examples are cited in Chapter 4.

people how many offences of different kinds they have *committed* can be extremely illuminating, but chiefly as bases for estimates of the percentages of certain groups of the population who have committed offences without detection. Because of the difficulties of sampling the population as a whole, special subgroups – such as schoolchildren, students, national servicemen – are chosen for sampling; nor do they usually know which of their offences were reported to the police – only which of them were not traced to the offender. Moreover, they may overstate or understate the extent of their wrongdoing, in both cases for obvious reasons.

A more relevant sort of investigation tries to sample not the potential offenders but the potential victims. The best example is the survey conducted throughout the USA by the National Opinion Research Centre of Chicago University (NORC), and described by Ennis (1967).

A battery of questionnaires was administered in the summer of 1966 to a 'national full multi-stage probability sample of 10,000 households in all parts of the continental United States', i.e. a sample so designed that every household had an equal chance of being included.

An adult (a person at least eighteen years old or a younger married person) in each of these households was given a twenty-minute 'screening interview' to see if anyone in the household had been a victim of any crime within the previous twelve months. A half-hour intensive interview was then held with each victim so identified, although if two or more persons had been victims in the same incident only one was interviewed. Interview schedules gave descriptions of eighteen crimes in layman's language. Interviewers were told to include attempts. If an incident involved more than one crime against the same victim (e.g. rape and robbery) only the most serious was to be counted. The interview sought to establish the nature of the crime, the extent and nature of losses, injuries or damage, whether the police had been told, any judicial outcome, and whatever descriptions of the offender were available. The result was an 'incident form' which was later checked by two independent 'evaluators' to make sure that the incident ought to be counted as a crime for the purpose of the survey. (Later an independent team of lawyers and detectives independently evaluated the incident forms, and agreed substantially with the original evaluators in 75 per cent to 80 per cent of the cases.)

The interviewed victims were also given a half-hour questionnaire to probe their attitudes about police, personal and neighbourhood security, and crime; and so was a random sample of non-victims, for comparative purposes.

Finally, a brief self-administered questionnaire was left in all the 'victim' and 'non-victim' households surveyed: it repeated the list of crimes used in the screening interview and was to be completed by the interviewed adults in the household in order to check the accuracy of the information given by the interviewed adult.

Table 1

Comparison of Survey and Officially Recorded Rates
(per 100,000 population)

Index Crimes	NORC survey 1965–6	UCR rate for individuals 1965*	UCR rate for individuals and organizations 1965*
Wilful homicide	3·0	5·1	5·1
Forcible rape	42·5	11·6	11·6
Robbery	94·0	61·4	61·4
Aggravated assault	218·3	106·6	106·6
Burglary	949·1	299·6	605·3
Larceny ($50 and over)	606·5	267·4	393·3
Motor vehicle theft	206·2	226·0	251·0
Total violence	357·8	184·7	184·7
Total property	1761·8	793·0	1249·6

* *Uniform Crime Reports*, Federal Bureau of Investigation, 1965, p. 51. The UCR national totals do not distinguish crimes committed against individuals or households from those committed against businesses or other organizations. The UCR rate for individuals is the published national rate adjusted to eliminate burglaries, larcenies and vehicle thefts not committed against individuals or households. No adjustment was made for robbery.

The main findings were summarized in two tables, reproduced here as Tables 1 and 2, which show considerable under-reporting of most of the crimes covered, for a variety of interesting reasons.

Results such as this are valuable as long as they are not made the basis of spuriously precise estimates. It would be quite unjustifiable to use Table 2, for example, to support the statement that 35 per cent

Table 2

Victims' Most Important Reason for not Notifying the Police* (in percentages)

Crimes	% cases in which police not notified	Reasons for not notifying the police					
		Felt it was private matter or did not want to harm offender	Police could not be effective or would not want to be bothered	Did not want to take time	Too confused or did not know how to report	Fear of reprisal
Robbery	35	27	45	9	18	0
Aggravated assault	35	50	25	4	8	13
Simple assault	54	50	35	4	4	7
Burglary	42	30	63	4	2	2
Larceny ($50 and over)	40	23	62	7	7	0
Larceny (under $50)	63	31	58	7	3	‡
Auto theft	11	20†	60†	0†	0†	20†
Malicious mischief	62	23	68	5	2	2
Consumer fraud	90	50	40	0	10	0
Other fraud (bad checks, swindling, etc.)	74	41	35	16	8	0
Sex offences (other than forcible rape)	49	40	50	0	5	5
Family crimes (desertion, non-support, etc.)	50	65	17	10	0	7

Source: NORC survey.

* Wilful homicide, forcible rape and a few other crimes had too few cases to be statistically useful, and they are therefore excluded.
† There were only five instances in which auto theft was *not* reported.
‡ Less than 0·5 per cent.

of robberies are not notified to the police, or even that 35 per cent of robberies in the USA were not notified to the police in the year of the survey. This would assume that both the sampling and the technique used to elicit the information were highly successful, whereas, as we have seen, they had defects.[2] What would be more justifiable would be a comparative statement to the effect that in the USA at the date in question serious crimes such as robbery and aggravated assault seemed to have a higher 'reportability' than less serious ones such as larcenies or malicious mischief.

Organizations as Victims

More problems arise when the victim is not a person but an organization, since those persons who are prepared to answer questions on its behalf may not be the persons most likely to know about offences against the organization. Nevertheless, there have been studies of this sort. J. P. Martin, for example, asked ninety-seven firms in the Reading, Berkshire, area for details of the six most recent cases of offences by employees which they could recall. The offences ranged from pilfering of petty sums or articles to thefts involving values of between £500 and £1000, and included thefts from the firm, from customers and from fellow-workers, as well as a few offences of sex and violence. None of the offences of violence had led to prosecutions, and more than half of the thefts had not. The smaller firms seemed even less likely than the larger ones to report their offenders, perhaps because their relations with their employees were closer. The firms' reasons for wanting to keep their cases out of court were very varied: triviality, dislike of publicity, of 'unpleasantness', of 'waste of time', liking for the employee and other explanations (see Martin, 1962).

2. The problems of sampling and eliciting information are the subject of an enormous technical literature, to which excellent introductions are Conways (1967) and Oppenheim (1966).

Chapter 2
Recorded Offences

When we turn to offences which *are* recorded we enter the realm of routine statistics. It is true that in some countries the only transactions recorded (apart from trials and their results) are 'arrests', which are one step further removed from real life. But well-organized systems for collecting criminal statistics usually manage to yield information about recorded cases in which the more serious crimes are reported to or observed by the police. In the USA, for example, the Federal Bureau of Investigation compiles *Uniform Crime Reports* which enumerate criminal homicides, forcible rapes, robberies, assaults, burglaries, larcenies and auto thefts that have been recorded by any of the 40,000 odd police forces in the country.

Let us concentrate, however, on the published annual *Criminal Statistics, England and Wales* (HMSO), which will henceforward be called the '*Criminal Statistics*'. (The Home Office also compile annual *Supplementary Criminal Statistics* which are not on sale, but are obtainable by libraries and research establishments from the Home Office's Statistical Division.) These consist of an Introductory Note, tables comparing the current with previous years, and annual tables; but essentially they are the result of counting either (*a*) transactions by police, whether these consist of recording reported offences or deciding that an offence has been 'cleared up'; or (*b*) proceedings in criminal courts.

There are a few minor tables which count a miscellaneous collection of subsidiary events,[1] but with these exceptions all the information in

1. Appeals against conviction or sentence (Tables V, VII), non-criminal proceedings in summary courts (Table VI), prosecutions by the Director of Public Prosecutions (Table X), cases involving extradition and fugitive offenders (Table XI and XII), hospital admissions and discharges of offenders subject to orders under Part V of the Mental Health Act 1959 (Tables XIII, XIV and XV), cases involving the exercise of the prerogative of mercy (Table XVI) and the use of legal aid in criminal proceedings (Table XVII).

the *Criminal Statistics* consists of different groupings of events of type (*a*) or (*b*). What might be called the substantive tables are those which show:

1. Indictable offences 'known to the police' (Table A).
2. Indictable offences 'cleared up' (Table A).
3. Indictable offences dealt with by a 'police caution' (Appendix III(*b*)).
4. Indictable offences tried at Assizes and Quarter Sessions, with the outcomes (Tables II and III).
5. Indictable and non-indictable offences tried summarily, with the outcomes (Table I).
6. 'Additional' (as distinct from 'principal') findings of guilt for indictable offences (Chapter V of the Introductory Note).

Note that what is being counted is in every case *transactions* (such as the reporting of an offence) and not natural events (such as a domestic fight) or offenders (for example, an aggressive husband). Many of these transactions involve the reappearance of offenders who have already offended and been detected, cautioned or tried (as the case may be) earlier in the same year.

Offences 'Known to the Police'

The rest of this chapter deals with the first of these types of transaction: indictable offences recorded as 'known to the police'. These have been published annually since 1857[2] and will be found in Table A, subdivided into certain groups, which will be discussed on page 69. Note that this table does *not* enumerate:

1. Most non-indictable offences, because to do so would greatly increase the labour involved. But some non-indictable offences are considered important enough to be included.

2. Incidents which are reported to the police as breaches of the criminal law, but which the police decide not to regard as offences. For example, because a child under the age of criminal liability cannot be found guilty of any offence, breaches of the criminal law by children in this age group used not to be (but now are) recorded as crimes made

2. With a break during the 1939–45 war (but grouped figures for this period were published in 1947).

known, but were included in a special monthly report to the Home Office. Again, a woman may report to a police station that her dog has been stolen; but if the police think it more likely that it has simply gone astray they will not record the incident as a theft.

3. Indictable offences which are neither observed by nor reported to the police, for reasons which have been discussed in Chapter 1.

Problems of Counting

Even when the police know of and decide to record an instance of criminal behaviour, counting often presents problems, some of which can be solved logically, others only in some arbitrary way. In an effort to ensure that they are at least solved in a *uniform* way by every police force, the Home Office's Statistical Division lays down rules in its unpublished *Instructions for the Preparation of Statistics Relating to Crime* (which libraries and research establishments can obtain from the Home Office).

Examples of the problems and their solutions are:

1. A commits what at first seems to the police to be a malicious wounding, but is later convicted of a mere assault. Should the incident be recorded as the former or the latter? The rule is that unless the incident eventually has to be written off as 'no crime' its original classification should not be altered. This holds even if A is acquitted. The exception is murder: if A is originally charged with murder but later convicted only of manslaughter the figures for 'murders known to the police' are corrected.[3] The justification for the exception is the desire for the greatest possible accuracy in counting the relatively small number of murders, in order to measure trends and assess the effect of changes in the penalty for this crime.

2. An anarchist kills two people with one bomb. A referee is attacked by ten spectators. An advertiser causes a fraudulent advertisement to appear in sixteen issues of *The Times* and defrauds eighty people. A father has sexual intercourse with his daughter ten times before his crime comes to light. A postman steals letters which he should have delivered to twenty-seven householders. A cashier pockets small sums

3. But note that the murder figures in Chapter V of the Introductory Note to the *Criminal Statistics* are even more elaborately corrected, as is explained there.

of money each week. A burglar breaks into a hotel and takes property from ten guests. How many crimes are involved in each case? The main rule for violent and sexual crimes is 'one victim, one crime', so that the anarchist commits two murders, one assault is committed on the referee and the father is guilty of only one crime of incest. In the USA, the *Uniform Crime Reports* use a similar rule. When it comes to the property offences, however, this rule is often modified, presumably because if rigidly applied it would give an exaggerated impression of the volume of crime (and perhaps because it would cause extra work for the police). The Perks Committee, which reported on the *Criminal Statistics* in 1967 was not altogether satisfied with the current rules, and proposed improvements (see Appendix C, pages 144ff.); but these have not yet been put into effect. The rule followed in the USA's *Uniform Crime Reports* for property offences is 'one operation, one crime', but this too leads to problems in practice.

3. Suppose that several crimes of different sorts are committed in the same operation: for instance, that a robbery is reported in which a man is shot. The rule in the USA is that the most serious of the crimes is counted, but not the others. No clear rule has been laid down in England.

Increasing 'Reportability'

Because the relative proportions of recorded and unrecorded crimes are unknown, fluctuations from year to year in these figures must be taken with a pinch of salt. This is especially true of *rising* trends, since some of the apparent increase may be due to increased readiness on the part of the public to report crime, or to increased efficiency on the part of the police in observing the commission of some sorts of crime. It is said, for example, that a large part of the apparent increase in crimes of violence must be attributed to increased reporting. The theory is that many of them occur in areas and groups in which antagonism to the police used to be so great that the idea of calling them in was repugnant, but that as middle-class attitudes percolate downwards so this antagonism decreases, and an increasing percentage of the violence which actually occurs is reported. It must be admitted that the evidence for this is scanty. For example, if this were so it might be predicted that the more serious the injury the smaller the increase would be. For murder usually leaves a body, and serious bodily harm usually leads to hospitalization and hospitals usually tell the police if the injury seems to have been inflicted criminally. If so, we should expect the minor assaults to give most scope for illusory increases due to increased reporting (see Figure 1). Certainly in this century figures for recorded malicious woundings have increased much faster than figures for more serious woundings, which in turn have increased faster than figures for murder: an observation which is consistent with[4] the theory that personal violence is increasing in 'reportability'. The same seems to be true of heterosexual offences. Table 3 gives the figures for rape, indecent assault on a female and unlawful intercourse with girls under thirteen and girls under sixteen for selected years from the beginning of this century (incest is omitted because it was not a criminal offence at the beginning of the century). If we assume that (a) the less serious sexual crimes were more markedly under-reported than the more serious; and (b) under-reporting is diminishing, we should predict that the increases would be sharper in indecent assaults than in rapes, and sharper in intercourse with girls

Table 3

Increases in Certain Recorded Heterosexual Offences

Year	Rape	Indecent assault on a female	Unlawful intercourse with	
			girl under 13	girl under 16
1900–1904 (average)	217	695	142	130
1938	99	2593	80	477
1948	252	5659	100	784
1961	503	9386	229	3923
1963	422	9641	190	4178
1967	702	11,369	295	4517
1967 figures as percentage of 1900–1904	323%	1640%	208%	3470%

4. It is also, of course, consistent with other possibilities: for example, that police are treating more and more reported violence as indictable. Both possibilities are probable.

26   Recorded Offences

under sixteen than in intercourse with girls under thirteen. This is what seems to have happened.

Another illusory sort of fluctuation occurs when police forces decide to devote more (or less) attention to a certain sort of crime. 'Gross indecency between males' appeared to increase steadily during the early 1950s. The Wolfenden Committee on Homosexual Offences and Prostitution was appointed in August 1954. By 1956 it was common

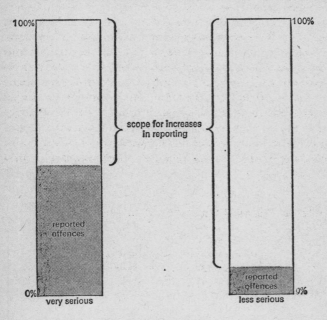

Figure 1 The hypothesis of differential scope for increased reporting

knowledge amongst people concerned with law enforcement that the Committee were opposed to the use of the criminal law to interfere with the private homosexual behaviour of adults, and the number of recorded offences had begun to fall, until by 1966 it had fallen to less than half its peak level of 1955. No change in the law had taken place, but police had been discouraged from enforcing it with too much zeal.

Finally, changes in counting rules lead to illusory fluctuations. For example, until 1950 the police returns to the Home Office were based

Increases in Certain Recorded Heterosexual Offences   27

on the offence of which the offender was ultimately found guilty (if he was). The result was that an offence which was originally treated as an indictable wounding might eventually be classified as a non-indictable assault, with the result that it would not figure in the return of crimes made known at all, because non-indictable assaults were not on the standard list. In 1950, however, the Home Office instructed police that (murder apart) whatever the offence with which the offender was eventually charged, or of which he was eventually convicted, it should be the offence which was originally thought to have been committed which should govern what was recorded in the 'crimes made known' report. We do not know what effect this had on the statistics as a whole, but so far as crimes of violence are concerned it has been estimated (by McClintock, 1963) that this alone would have inflated the 1938 figures for the London Metropolitan area by 7·5 per cent. Other minor reforms – mostly by way of greater uniformity between police forces – would have brought the total of illusory increase due to changes in recording practice up to about 13·5 per cent.

It seems most unlikely, however, that the marked increase in recorded reports of many types of crime over the last half century can be entirely explained away on these lines. In all probability there has been a considerable increase in at least the more serious forms of violence and acquisitive crime. With slightly less confidence the same could be said of heterosexual offences against unwilling victims.

Chapter 3
Cleared-Up Offences

The sorts of figures with which we shall be concerned in this chapter differ in one important way from those which we have so far been considering. Statistics of 'cleared-up offences' are more accurate than those of 'offences known to the police' since the former reflect transactions in which the police themselves are involved, whereas the police may not be witnesses to the latter.[1] The most unsatisfactory feature of 'offences known to the police' thus more or less disappears when we turn to 'cleared-up offences' and the statistics of appearances in criminal courts.

Here again, it is important to be sure what is being counted and according to what rules.

1. Obviously an offence is 'cleared up' by the police if they trace it to a suspect who is then prosecuted and convicted. But there are other circumstances in which they are also allowed, indeed instructed, to classify the offence as 'cleared up'.

2. An offender who pleads or is found guilty of an offence is allowed to ask the court to 'take into consideration' (t.i.c.) other similar offences which he has committed when it is deciding upon its sentence. The effect of this is that the court will take account of these offences when deciding upon his sentence and that he will not be prosecuted for them even if the police later obtain sufficient evidence to convict him; so that he is able to protect himself against a series of prosecutions while he is, let us say, serving a prison sentence for the offence for which he has been successfully prosecuted. In practice, the police will often present a thief or housebreaker whom they are prosecuting with a list of other property offences, and ask him if he is willing to have any of

1. This is not to deny that there are unfortunately local variations in the rules for counting offences as cleared up; but these are gradually being eliminated.

them t.i.c. Prisoners sometimes say that in return they are promised that the police will give favourable – or less unfavourable – evidence about their antecedents at the sentencing stage; police deny this. However that may be, an offence which has been t.i.c. is officially cleared up. Similarly, a prisoner serving a sentence sometimes admits to an offence for which the police do not think it worth prosecuting him; and this, too, is treated as 'cleared up'. Table VI of the *Supplementary Criminal Statistics* shows, for each type of principal offence (see the glossary) the numbers of offences t.i.c.: they are common in the case of property offences, fairly rare in other cases.

3. An awkwardness arises when an offence has obviously been committed by several people (e.g. an attack on someone) but only one is identified and prosecuted. In such cases the offence is treated as cleared up, even though the majority of those responsible have not been brought to justice, or even identified.

4. More controversial is the ruling[2] that if a person is arrested or summoned for an offence, it is cleared up even if he is later acquitted or if the prosecution is dropped. These cases present an awkward problem. For an acquittal can mean:

(i) that the jury (or magistrates) decided that the police might well have charged the wrong person, and that someone else was responsible for the offence;

(ii) that they accepted that the accused was the person responsible for the act or omission charged, but did not regard him as legally guilty beyond reasonable doubt, either (*a*) because of doubts about the necessary mental element (e.g. whether the alleged shoplifter really intended to leave the shop without paying), or (*b*) because of doubts as to whether the act or omission charged was in fact a breach of the criminal law;

(iii) that the jury (or the magistrates, although they are usually more hard-hearted than juries) had no reasonable doubts that the act or omission was a breach of the law, or that the necessary mental conditions were fulfilled, but simply thought that it would be too hard on the accused to convict him and punish him (for juries seldom say to

2. In the Home Office's *Instructions for the Preparation of Statistics Relating to Crime.*

themselves, 'If we convict he is certain to get off with a discharge or a binding over'; and indeed how can they safely assume this?).

In cases (ii) and (iii) it is obviously sensible to treat the acquittal as irrelevant to the question whether the offence should be treated as cleared up. But in case (i), where the reason for the acquittal was reasonable doubt as to whether the right person had been prosecuted, it is arguable that it should not be regarded as cleared up. On the other hand, consider two points:

(i) Reasonable doubt that it was the right person does not mean 'probably it was someone else'; it is quite consistent with a belief that it probably was the right person who was accused; and the police are often in the position of having better evidence that it was the right person than they are able to bring into court.

(ii) In any case, it is often impossible to know the true reason for an acquittal – especially if the trial is before a jury, who must not be interrogated.

So while the ruling that an offence is cleared up even if the prosecution has failed or been withdrawn is a rough and ready one, it is not unreasonable.

5. Nor is it unreasonable to regard the case as cleared up if:

(i) 'the guilt of the offender is clear, but the person offended against refuses to, or is permanently unable to, or (if a juvenile) is not permitted by whoever is in charge of him, to give evidence'; or if essential witnesses are dead;

(ii) 'the offender admits an offence, but there is a definite obstacle to proceedings' (e.g. if in a case of theft no precise sum of money can be specified owing to bad book-keeping);

(iii) the offender has simply been cautioned by the police (as often happens where the offender is a child without a record; see Chapter 5);

(iv) if the offender has died, or been removed to a mental hospital before proceedings were instituted.

6. Finally, if the crime turns out to have been committed by a child under the age of criminal liability, it is now treated as cleared up. Until the end of 1968, however, the rule was that the incident should be written off as 'no crime'. This was not only illogical (since offences recorded but not cleared up must have included many by under-age children) but also slightly impaired the comparability of figures for

periods when the age of criminal liability was different (it was raised from seven to eight in 1933, and from eight to ten in 1964).

Clear-Up Rates as a Police Efficiency Index

Table A of the *Criminal Statistics* allows us to compare the numbers of indictable offences made known to the police with the numbers cleared up. There is an inevitable tendency to regard the percentages of offences which are cleared up as an index of the efficiency of different police forces, or of the same force over different periods. But there are pitfalls here. In the first place, some types of offence are much easier to clear up than others. Personal violence as can be seen by looking at, say, offence groups 5 and 8,[3] is cleared up in more than 80 per cent of cases; and murder, whether attempted or successful, even more often. The reason is partly that the police take more trouble over personal violence than over most other sorts of crime; but mainly that in many cases of violence the victim knows his or her assailant personally. McClintock (1963), p. 80 shows how much difference this makes to clear-up rates:

Were the participants previously known to each other?	1950 % cleared up	1957 % cleared up
Yes	97% of 615	96% of 943
No	69% of 423	62% of 835
Total	85% of 1038	80% of 1778

Contrast with these figures the very low clear-up percentage for, say, larceny from unattended vehicles, which in 1967 was only 22 per cent. This is a type of crime which the police rightly regard as little more than a nuisance. The property stolen – radios, typewriters, cameras, binoculars, cartons of cigarettes or crates of spirits – is easy to dispose of profitably, and hard to trace. A large number of police man-hours spent on these petty thefts would yield very little in the way of property recovered or thieves caught. To some extent, too, the police feel that

3. For a fuller description of the offences in each group, see Appendix IV of the *Criminal Statistics*.

the drivers of the vehicles are to blame for their carelessness, and that the theft is being reported in order to satisfy the requirements of insurance companies rather than in any hope of recovering the stolen property. Often the most that can be done is to file a description of readily identifiable articles in the local or national index of stolen goods.

On the other hand, some kinds of petty theft have what is at first sight a remarkably high clear-up rate. 'Larceny from shops and stalls' (group 46) appears to be cleared-up in 79 per cent of cases. This is a spurious percentage, however, because shoplifting is not usually reported to the police unless the shoplifter is caught. If the figure of shopliftings made known to the police were nearer the true figure of shopliftings actually committed, the cleared-up shopliftings would be a much smaller percentage of the total. Indeed, this being so, what really requires some explanation is the 21 per cent of cases which apparently were *not* cleared up. Most of them probably involved articles of considerable value, and were reported in order to satisfy the requirements of insurance policies.

If therefore one is going to use clear-up rates as an index of police efficiency, it is important to exclude, so far as possible, types of offence which are usually (*a*) reported only when a suspect is identified (e.g. shoplifting) or (*b*) regarded as a mere nuisance by police (e.g. thefts from parked cars).

Indeed, it would probably be best to select a type of offence which the police are known to take seriously, but in which the circumstances do not point to a particular suspect. The best example for which we have figures is crimes of violence in which the offender was a stranger to the victim. McClintock enables us to compare the clear-up percentages for such crimes for the years 1950 and 1957:

	1950	1957	
Sexual	53% of 43	55% of 91	
Pub and café disputes	78% of 110	62% of 77	
Street disputes	62% of 189	59% of 406	$p < 0.01$ [4]
Misc. attacks	86% of 22	68% of 25	
Civilians intervening	80% of 59	76% of 108	
Total	69% of 423	62% of 319	$p < 0.05$ [4]

4. See pages 88–9 for an explanation of p.

There seems to have been a slight decrease in all the clear-up rates, with the exception of sexual attacks for which it has remained steady. The numbers in McClintock's sample, however, are rather small, and most of these small differences are not significant (see Chapter 11).

Unfortunately no similar figures have been published for more recent years. Another category of crime, however, which will serve equally well as an index of efficiency in clearing up offences is robbery, since the police take this seriously, regarding it as a 'professional's' crime. Table 4 shows the crude figures of robberies 'made known' to and 'cleared up' by the police from 1950 to 1967, and also the latter as percentages of the former.

Table 4

Robberies Reported to and 'Cleared Up' by Police, England and Wales

Year	(a) Robberies 'made known to police'	(b) 'Cleared up'	(c) Column (b) as % of column (a)
1950	1021	527	51·7
1951	800	373	46·7
1952	1002	523	52·2
1953	980	510	52·1
1954	812	418	51·5
1955	823	432	52·5
1956	965	477	49·4
1957	1194	573	48·0
1958	1692	788	46·6
1959	1900	879	46·2
1960	2014	933	46·3
1961	2349	922	39·3
1962	2517	1076	42·7
1963	2483	1069	42·9
1964	3066	1182	38·6
1965	3736	1378	36·9
1966	4474	1662	37·2
1967	4564	1837	40·4
1968	4815	1902	39·5

Source: Table A of the *Criminal Statistics*.

Two points must be made here. One is that although the *percentages* have fallen the *actual numbers* of robberies cleared up have risen. It is not that the police are solving less, but that the numbers of reported robberies are rising faster than the numbers which they solve.

'Immunity'

Secondly, we cannot infer from clear-up rates how many offenders are never caught. For these rates refer to single offences, and only if no offender ever committed more than one offence would they enable the number of undetected offenders to be estimated. This is not, of course, how most offenders behave. Thieves, bad drivers, sexual offenders and to a lesser extent people who break the law in other ways usually do so more than once. Taking the case of thieves, let us make the artificial (and, of course, over-optimistic) assumption that, in general, a thief's chance of getting away with a single theft (what is called his 'immunity') is 50 per cent. If he commits two thefts, his chances are 50 per cent of 50 per cent, that is, 25 per cent. If he commits three, his chances are 50 per cent of 25 per cent, and so on: a geometric progression. In fact, as McClintock and Avison point out (1968, p. 123) the general immunity for a single offence is usually a good deal higher than the clear-up rate by itself would suggest, since – at least so far as acquisitive offences are concerned – many are cleared up only when another offence has been cleared up and the offender either admits to them or is found in possession of the stolen goods. McClintock and Avison, therefore, talk in terms of a general immunity for a single acquisitive offence of about 75 per cent. And to be more realistic still there must be acquisitive offenders whose skill gives them greater-than-average immunity (which may even increase with experience so far as *single* offences are concerned, although it cannot but decline for the whole series of their offences). Nevertheless, the fact remains that the more offences one commits the lower one's over-all immunity must become.

Chapter 4
The Prevalence of Law-Breaking and Convictions

What has just been said about the declining immunity of habitual offenders should not be allowed to obscure the fact that there must be considerable numbers of people who have committed occasional offences without detection. Several investigations have attempted to estimate the prevalence[1] of what is usually called 'hidden delinquency'.[2] One of the best known is that of Short and Nye (1957, pp. 207–13). They gave nearly 1200 high-school boys a long questionnaire, which was to be answered anonymously, and in which were scattered some questions about such offences as driving a car without a driver's licence, drug use, and theft. Considerable percentages of boys in all social classes admitted to these acts.

Two Scandinavian investigations which also relied on questionnaires are described (in English) in Christiansen (1965). A British investigation is described by Willcock and Stokes (1968) in a Government Social Survey Report. W. A. Belson *et al.* (1968) experimented with different techniques of questioning on a sample of 159 boys between the ages of twelve and seventeen in four 'widely different' polling districts of Greater London. Lynn McDonald questioned some 850 boys in the fourth forms of twelve schools, in different parts of London and the West Country. The technique used in all these British investigations was a private interview with each subject; indeed Dr Belson's investigation consisted of a series of questionings designed to see which method elicited most admissions. The aim in most cases was to find out how many of the subjects had *at any time in their lives* committed offences of various kinds, and how many of these had

1. For the precise meaning of 'prevalence' and the distinction between it and 'incidence', see Glossary of Technical Terms, page 139.

2. 'Hidden delinquency' must be distinguished from the 'dark figure' of unreported offences, which was discussed in Chapter 1.

resulted in detection, with its possible consequences. All of them appeared to reveal a considerable amount of undetected law-breaking, most of it petty, but some of it more serious.

There is at least one interesting difference between the English results, based on interviews, and the Scandinavian and American ones, based on questionnaires: the former indicate a significant difference between social classes in the prevalence and frequency of law breaking, while the latter suggest that social-class differences are not great. Some users of questionnaires – for example, Short and Nye in the article cited – have used their results in an attempt to undermine official statistics which suggest that the lower occupational groups are responsible for proportionately more law breaking. Since questionnaires about detected and undetected law breaking show only slight differences between classes, it is argued that the process of detection, prosecution and so forth which leads to conviction is biased in favour of the middle and upper classes. Without denying the existence of such a bias it must be pointed out that the results of English *interviews* support rather than undermine the impression that law breaking is more frequent amongst the lower social classes. Unless we are to suppose that this is an English phenomenon, and that differences in social class in the USA and Scandinavia are much less strongly associated with law breaking, it seems reasonable to conclude that the interview method yields more realistic results.

The inevitable defects of both methods, however, must not be overlooked. In the first place, the subjects of nearly all these investigations were schoolchildren, and the remaining few were based on samples of university students or other very young adults. Consequently, most of the prevalence of law breaking was accounted for by adolescent misbehaviour. I know of no modern survey designed to estimate the prevalence of undetected adult law breaking. In the second place, however sophisticated the techniques it was almost impossible for the investigators to protect themselves against three sources of error: the subjects who refuse to take part (and who probably include a high percentage of law-breakers), the subjects who take part but conceal their misdeeds and those who take part but exaggerate their misdeeds out of frivolity or bravado.

The Prevalence of Law-Breaking and Convictions   37

The Prevalence of Past Convictions

A different, but equally important, problem is the estimation of the prevalence of convictions: that is, of the numbers of people in a population who have at any time in their careers been found guilty of offences. The practical importance of having some idea of this figure was demonstrated when the Morris Committee was considering the possibility that a jury might include people who had in the past been convicted, and who might therefore be biased in favour of the accused. The Committee was told that when the names of thirty-eight jurors at the Old Bailey had been checked a year or so earlier it had been found that four certainly had convictions serious enough to appear in the Criminal Records Office (CRO) files (see Chapter 13), while nine others 'appeared' to have criminal records (the explanation of the uncertainty was probably that the investigators did not have the information necessary to make sure that two people of the same name had not been confused). Although the Committee was assured that the juries in question had returned reasonable verdicts, it took the situation seriously enough to recommend the changes in the law which now disqualify certain ex-prisoners – although not all convicted persons – from jury service.

Since convictions are officially recorded, it would seem a fairly easy matter to sample the population in which one is interested and then find out how many members of it have criminal records: this is what the investigators of the thirty-eight Old Bailey jurymen were doing in a very rough and ready way. In practice, as we shall see, there are difficulties, and the only respectable investigation of this kind known to me is a Danish one, described by Preben Wolf in Christiansen (1965). He found that in a sample of 3032 men who in 1953–4 were between their twentieth and seventieth birthdays, 10 per cent were listed in the official Danish registers as having committed breaches of the Penal Code (which correspond roughly to English indictable offences) and another 9 per cent were listed for breaches of 'special laws' (corresponding roughly to non-indictable offences). For various reasons he concluded that these were minimum figures, and that the percentage of people who ought, in consistency, to appear on the registers was higher. On the other hand, his figures included an unstated number whose only offence was committed when they were very young.

It must be pointed out, however, that it is no easy matter to collect a representative sample of people who have left school. Some groups – such as vagrants and seamen – are either hard to sample or tend to be uncooperative. Moreover, even the use of official records presents problems. In England, only indictable offences – plus a few selected non-indictable offences – are even required to be reported to the Criminal Records Office and the Home Office's Statistical Division; the rest are merely recorded (if at all) by the local police. Where juveniles are concerned the police do not always report even standard list offences to the central records, especially if the juvenile has merely been cautioned. To identify members of a large sample in the CRO files would not merely be a considerable burden to a hard-worked office; it would also raise problems of identification where common names are involved, unless the exact date of birth is known. The Home Office's Offenders' Index is in a form which would make the operation somewhat easier, but unfortunately it did not come into existence until the middle of the 1960s, so that it will not be usable *for this purpose* until it has been in operation for the average person's lifetime.

One or two attempts, however, have been made to arrive at estimates by less direct – and less accurate – methods. The best British example is the follow-up, by J. W. B. Douglas *et al.* (1967), of a cohort of boys born in the first week of March 1946. By their seventeenth birthdays, 2402 boys were still alive and traceable in this country. Using these the investigators estimated that by this age 14·6 per cent had been either cautioned or tried and sentenced for an offence; and 10·4[3] per cent had been found guilty of an indictable offence. A similar cohort study, in Philadelphia, was based on a follow-up of 10,000 boys who had been born in 1945 and had lived in the city between their tenth and eighteenth birthdays. By their eighteenth birthdays no less than 35 per cent had been in some sort of recorded trouble with the police.[4]

Until cohorts such as these have yielded information about law breaking by adults (and it must be remembered that the numbers of

3. These percentages would have been higher still if illegitimate children had not had to be excluded from the survey.

4. I am indebted to Professor M. E. Wolfgang for this information. The British and Philadelphian results are not, of course, comparable. The latter was confined to a city population, and included very minor infractions, as well as traffic offences.

traceable individuals dwindles year by year), we must rely for this purpose on a less satisfactory method. The *Supplementary Criminal Statistics* used to include a table (Table V) which showed, separately for age groups, the numbers of males and females convicted for the first time of a centrally recorded offence while in a given age group. Thus in 1965 the probabilities for males were apparently as shown in Table 5.

The table demonstrates the use of 'cumulative' percentages in the right-hand column, where the percentages represent the probability for the age group in question *plus* all the probabilities for earlier age groups. The method treats these cumulative percentages as a rough estimate of the number of males who by the age in question have at some time in their lives incurred a conviction for a centrally recorded offence. The method, however, has several defects. In the first place, the table in the *Supplementary Criminal Statistics* on which it is based is suspected of being unsound, in that a substantial number of offenders appear as 'first offenders' in more than one age group, because of delays in reporting and other difficulties: this seems particularly likely to occur where offences by persons under seventeen are concerned. Notice that the cumulative percentage (13·31) for the under-seventeen age group is substantially higher than the 10·4 per cent estimate arrived at by Douglas's method. It was partly for this reason that the Home Office discontinued the inclusion of Table V after 1963, at least for the time being. The other important defect is the assumption that the 1963 rates of first conviction had been constant during the life-times of each age group, although we know that conviction rates (and therefore probably first-conviction rates) have been rising fairly steeply. By the same token, the likelihood of future increases means that the 1963 rates are not a very sound basis for predicting the prevalence of convictions in, say, the population of the mid-seventies.

It is arguable that, in any case, this is one of those situations, fortunately frequent in the social sciences, in which it does not matter very much whether the correct percentage is 10·4, or 8·4 or 12·4. For practical purposes it is sufficient to establish that the percentage is very substantial. On the other hand, there are situations in which more precise estimates of conviction prevalence are needed. For example, T. C. Willett (1964) who took a sample of 653 traffic offenders from one of the Home Counties in the late 1950s, found that no less than 23 per cent of them had previous convictions for *non-motoring* offences

Table 5

Prevalence of Convictions for Centrally Recorded Offences amongst Males in 1963

Age group	(a) Males in age group to nearest 1000	(b) Males first convicted of standard list offences in 1963	(c) Column (b) as % of Column (a)	(d) Column (c) as cumulative percentage
8	331,000	717	0·22	0·22
9	339,000	1730	0·51	0·73
10	337,000	2804	0·83	1·56
11	328,000	3774	1·15	2·71
12	345,000	5637	1·63	4·34
13	354,000	7767	2·19	6·53
14	374,000	9880	2·62	9·15
15	398,000	8767	2·20	11·35
16	446,000	8728	1·96	13·31
17	342,000	7629	2·23	15·54
18	341,000	7178	2·11	17·65
19	346,000	5921	1·71	19·36
20	328,000	4786	1·46	20·82
21–4	1,204,000	14,351	1·19	22·01
25–9	1,512,000	11,174	0·74	22·75
30–39	3,087,000	13,307	0·43	23·18
40–49	3,130,000	8545	0·27	23·45
50–59	3,013,000	4117	0·14	23·59
60	3,308,000	1595	0·05	23·64

(including non-indictable offences) and concluded that there was an association between motoring offences and criminality. He did not, however, have the benefit of any sound estimate of the prevalence of convictions for non-motoring indictable and non-indictable offences. If he had, he would probably have found that so far as *bad drivers* were concerned his offenders had cleaner records than was to be expected (especially when allowance was made for differences in social class).[5]

5. It was offenders whose offence consisted of driving without insurance or while disqualified who accounted for most of the 'criminal records', and these were usually young male motor-cyclists from social classes with a higher than average conviction prevalence.

The Prevalence of Past Convictions 41

Chapter 5
Police Cautions

The next category of figures which the *Criminal Statistics* provide concerns what happens to the detected offenders. Most of them, of course, are brought to trial; but we must not forget that convenient power which the police have to deal with an offender – the 'caution' or 'warning'. (This is not to be confused of course with the 'cautions' which the police must administer in order to comply with Judges' Rules when they are questioning suspects.) In the sense with which we are concerned a caution means: (*a*) an interview with a senior police officer at which the offender is told that he will not be prosecuted for the offence this time, but will be if he commits another; or (*b*) a letter from the police to this effect.

A letter is the usual method of conveying a caution for a traffic offence; an interview is the usual way of conveying it in other cases; In theory a caution is used only for offences which are not regarded as serious, and which are committed by persons with clean records who admit their guilt, but in practice there are plenty of exceptions. For example, police sometimes caution in cases in which they know they would have difficulty in bringing a successful prosecution: see the monograph on police cautioning by Steer (1971).

So far as indictable offences are concerned, the chief use of cautions is in dealing with juvenile delinquents, and especially the younger ones. The last column of Appendix III(b) of the *Criminal Statistics* shows the cautioning rate per 100,000 persons of age ten, eleven and so on. If you compare this with Appendix III(a) you will see that in the first year of criminal liability more children are dealt with by caution than by being found guilty by a court, and so far as girls are concerned the same is true of age eleven. But the proportion of cautions to prosecutions declines steadily with advancing age, until it is lowest for the twenty-five to thirty age group. Then it rises slightly and for offenders over sixty it soars again. Those who are interested in the greater leniency with which women are treated by the penal system may find it interesting to compare the proportions for the two sexes.

For the numbers of *non-indictable* offences dealt with by cautions it is necessary to consult the *Supplementary Criminal Statistics*, Table VIII, which also subdivides the figures for both indictable and non-indictable offences according to offence groups and police areas.

Chapter 6
Judicial Statistics

This chapter is concerned with judicial statistics, or more precisely with criminal (as distinct from civil) judicial statistics; and in particular with those in the Home Office's published *Criminal Statistics*.

The annual judicial statistics for higher courts begin with the year 1834,[1] and were extended to summary courts in 1857. Separate tables for children and young persons were not published until 1910, although earlier volumes show the age groups of convicted offenders.

Being concerned with formal transactions in courts, these statistics are not subject to many of the sorts of inaccuracy which afflict the counting operations described in earlier chapters. Police forces have little difficulty in recording and reporting to the Home Office the nature of the offence for which an offender is prosecuted (since they are in most cases responsible for the wording of the charge), or the outcome. If uncertainty arises as to the precise sentence, they can ask the clerk of the court. Occasionally they miss a case: for example, when it is added to the court's 'agenda' at short notice, or when the prosecutor is an agency such as a local authority, as it is for instance when the offence involves weights or measures. Sometimes, too, they overlook the fact that the offender has been convicted of a lesser offence than that for which he was prosecuted. But such errors are not frequent.

Again it is important to realize what is not being counted. The judicial statistics do not count individual offenders; they count appearances by offenders in court. The same offender may appear more than once within the year, on the same or on a different sort of charge, and with different results. Nor do they count charges. A single appearance may involve more than one charge; if so the rule is that the police

1. A few special returns for earlier years can be found in the Parliamentary papers, but are not in the same form, and are almost certainly less reliable.

should report each offence charged, but that what is counted for the purpose of tabulation is the 'principal offence', as it is called. This means the offence for which the proceedings were carried to the furthest stage (for example, acquittal would be a stage beyond the abandonment of prosecution, and conviction would be a stage further still). If more than one charge led to conviction, the principal offence is the one for which the heaviest sentence[2] was imposed; and if the actual sentences were the same, it is the offence carrying the highest *permissible* sentence. Thus a man convicted of both indecent assault and theft at the same appearance and sentenced to twelve months' imprisonment for each would be counted as a thief because theft carried a heavier maximum penalty. (Yet note that if he were convicted at the same appearance of an indictable and a non-indictable offence, the appearance would be counted in the section of the tables dealing with non-indictable offences as well as in the section dealing with indictable offences.)

Some information, however, about 'non-principal offences' can be found in the Introductory Note to the *Criminal Statistics* (Chapter V) and in Table VII of the *Supplementary Criminal Statistics*. From the former, for example, it can be seen that about one in every four adult men and about one in five women who were found guilty of indictable offences were found guilty on more than one charge. The percentage seems to be even higher for juveniles, although it cannot be assumed that this tells us something about juvenile law breaking. For it is distinctly possible that a juvenile detected in a single offence is simply more likely than an adult to admit to additional offences.

'Non-principal offences' must of course be distinguished from offences t.i.c., which are not the subject of a charge, but which a person who has been found guilty on another charge can ask the court to take into consideration when passing sentence, so as to rule out any future prosecution for them (see page 29). Information about t.i.c. offences can be found in Table VI of the *Supplementary Criminal Statistics* where it can be seen, for example, how frequent it is for acquisitive offences and how rare for violent offences to be t.i.c.

2. A fine is treated as heavier than probation although, as we shall see in Chapter 12, there is some evidence that young males regard probation as more oppressive.

Acquittal Rates

A serious defect of the present judicial statistics from the lawyer's point of view is that they do not show how many appearances involved pleas of 'guilty'. Consequently, although they show acquittals, these cannot be related to numbers of 'not guilty' pleas, so that we can have no idea how many appearances involved a genuine trial of guilt or what the acquittal rate is for different offences. The only table of this kind so far published – so far as England is concerned – will be found in the *New Law Journal* for 9 June 1966; and even this deals only with trials at higher courts. The acquittal rates which it showed for different types of offence seemed startlingly high; but more recent figures for 1969 (with which the Home Office's Statistical Division have been kind enough to supply me) are even more striking:

Type of offence	Acquittal rate
Burglary and robbery	40%
Violence against the person[3]	41%
Sexual offences	57%
Fraud or handling stolen goods	57%
Theft[4]	60%
All types	50%

Although these acquittal rates are higher than those given in the *New Law Journal* for the mid-nineteen sixties (perhaps because of the increasing availability of legal aid) they exhibit similar differences between types of offence. The rates for violence and burglary are markedly lower than for sexual and acquisitive offences. One can only speculate about the reasons for this. Does the evidence of identification tend to be stronger in cases of violence or burglary (as we have seen on page 32, most victims of violence are personally acquainted with the assailant)? Or do the facts tend to leave less room for argument about the criminality of the act?

3. Excluding death or injury caused by motor vehicles.
4. Excluding thefts and unauthorized takings of motor vehicles.

Comparing Sentences

The main judicial tables are I(a) and II(a) (see pages 148–51, which show the results of appearances at magistrates' and higher courts respectively, for offenders of all ages. But, since magistrates' courts include juvenile courts, Table I(a) includes large numbers of appearances by children and young persons, which are negligible in the higher courts, as a glance at Tables II(d) and (e) will show. Even where 'young adults' of seventeen to twenty are concerned, comparisons are complicated by special sentences confined to this age group, and in some cases imposable only by higher courts, as Borstal training is, or only by lower courts, as attendance centre orders are. So when comparing what happens at higher and lower courts it is better to compare the tables for offenders aged twenty-one or older (Tables I(b) and II(b)).

The most important information in these tables is the distribution of courts' sentences between the various choices open to them. To compare the crude numbers involved, which differ from one type of court to another and from indictable offences to motoring and other non-indictable offences, would be almost meaningless; what is required is to reduce them to percentages of the totals of convictions. This is what has been done in Table 6, which shows how very different the pattern of sentencing is for higher and lower courts, and for the three main categories of offence. Fines, for instance, are the main weapon of summary courts, even for indictable offences, whereas in higher courts, imprisonment, immediate or suspended, takes their place.

Fallacious Comparisons

Is it possible to compare the severity with which courts approach different types of offence? Is it true, for instance, that they are harder on offences against property than on offences against the person? If we compare men of twenty-one or older sentenced by higher courts in 1968 for shopbreaking with those sentenced for 'malicious wounding' we find that 62 per cent of the former received immediate sentences of imprisonment, compared with only 52 per cent of the latter. But it would be fallacious to infer from this, as is sometimes done, that we are a nation of shopkeepers, and that judges and recorders have more regard for property than for persons. For the tables unfortunately do not distinguish between 'first offenders' and offenders who, having criminal records, tend to receive more severe sentences. Shopbreakers tend to have criminal records more often than men convicted of violence, and this would probably account for the apparently greater

Table 6

Methods by which Offenders of Both Sexes Aged Twenty-One or Older were Dealt with by English Courts or Police in 1968

Method of dealing with the offender*	Indictable offences		Non-indictable offences	
	Assizes and Quarter Sessions	Magistrates' courts	Magistrates' courts	
			Non-motoring	Motoring
	%†	%†	%†	%†
Absolute discharge	n	1	1	1
Conditional discharge	3	13	3	n
Recognizance	n	n	1	—
Probation	10	8	1	n
Fine	11	53	90	98
Suspended sentence	21	14	2	n
Immediate imprisonment	53	8	2	n
Hospital order	2	n	n	n
Otherwise dealt with	n	4‖	n	n
Total dealt with by courts	24,488‡§	117,830‡	262,751‡	818,425‡
Cautioned by police		5889‡	16,903‡	272,061‡

n = negligible, i.e. less than 0·5 per cent.

* The table does not reflect with complete accuracy the relative frequencies with which each measure is used because, as we have seen, the figures on which it is based reflect only cases in which the measure in question was the heaviest. What are shown are, therefore, the relative frequencies of cases in which each measure was the most severe measure applied to the offender.

† Since percentages are given as whole numbers, they do not always total 100 per cent.

‡ Since individuals may be dealt with more than once in the same year, these figures represent occasions and not individuals. For example, only 242,709 individuals were cautioned for motoring offences.

§ Including persons sentenced at higher courts after conviction at lower courts.

‖ Nearly all committed to Quarter Sessions for sentence.

severity with which they are sentenced. The only sound comparison would be confined to 'first offenders' convicted of both sorts of offence (see pages 60–61).

The same fallacy can easily be committed when comparing sentencing policies of courts at different dates, for the characteristics of offenders which influence sentencers may be differently distributed in different 'vintages'. This can be illustrated (see Table 7) by figures taken from McClintock (1963, p. 165).[5]

Table 7

Sentences Imposed on Adults over Twenty-One for Violent Crimes in the London Metropolitan Police District

Sentence	All offenders		'First offenders'		With non-violent records		With violent records	
	1957 %	1960 %	1957 %	1960 %	1957 %	1960 %	1957 %	1960 %
Prison*	40†	38	18	18	51	43†	64	72
Probation	3	6	4	9	4	6	2	—
Fine	36	35	49	43	30	37	23	18
Nominal	20	21	29	30	15	15	11	10
$N(=100\%)$	989	1192	423	556	315	348	251	288

*Including a few other institutional measures.

† Since percentages are given as whole numbers, they do not always total 100 per cent.

If all that is compared are the figures for 'all offenders', the impression gained is that there was little change in the sentencing policy of London courts between 1957 and 1960. But if they are subdivided into 'first offenders', offenders with non-violent records, and offenders with violent records the picture changes. Courts seem to have become tougher with offenders who had violent records, more lenient with the rest.

Effect of a New Measure

If the years are very close together, of course, and the numbers which are being compared are very large, it is unlikely that there will have

5. McClintock himself did not, of course, commit this fallacy.

been a sharp change in the percentage of recidivists coming up for sentence. Thus it is possible to study the effect of the introduction of the suspended prison sentence in 1968 without worrying about this fallacy. All that is necessary is to compare the distribution of sentences in 1968 and 1969 with those for the immediately preceding years, as is done in Table 8. This shows clearly that so far as indictable offences

Table 8

The Effect of Introducing the Suspended Sentence on the Disposal of Men Aged Twenty-One or Older*

	Total found guilty	Discharges and recog- nizances	Probation	Fines	Suspended imprison- ment	Immediate imprison- ment
		(Shown as percentages † of totals found guilty)				
Higher courts						
1964	13,667*	6·1	13·8	21·2	—	57·2
1965	14,803*	5·3	13·2	24·5	—	55·5
1966	16,042*	4·3	11·6	23·8	—	59·0
1967	16,896*	5·4	12·6	24·5	—	56·3
1968	17,674*	3·9	8·7	14·0	21·8	50·2
1969	20,951*	4·2	7·8	14·5	20·8	51·4
Magistrates' courts: indictable offences						
1964	71,476	9·4	8·1	57·8	—	18·9
1965	76,941	8·5	7·9	60·2	—	17·9
1966	85,577	8·2	7·6	60·9	—	17·9
1967	90,362	9·3	8·4	61·8	—	15·1
1968	96,660	9·7	6·3	52·7	16·2	9·5
1969	112,664	9·8	6·2	55·0	14·5	9·6
Magistrates' courts: non-indictable, non-motoring offences						
1964	204,605	3·9	0·7	91·6	—	3·0
1965	197,134	3·9	0·8	91·1	—	3·2
1966	204,540	4·1	0·8	91·3	—	3·3
1967	225,433	4·3	0·8	91·7	—	2·8
1968	234,577	4·5	0·8	90·5	1·8	1·8
1969	252,758	4·3	0·6	91·6	1·2	1·4

* Excluding men committed to higher courts for sentence only.

† Since numerically insignificant measures (such as hospital orders) are not included, the percentages do not total 100 per cent.

are concerned both higher and lower courts used the suspended sentence not only for men whom they would in the previous year have imprisoned, but also for men whom they would previously have fined: for the use of both immediate imprisonment and fines dropped sharply. But the table also illustrates the desirability of taking not merely the year before and the year after a change, but a series of years; for only by doing so can one see whether there is the awkward possibility that any changes in percentages were simply part of a long-term trend. For example, did the suspended sentence also replace some probation orders and some discharges in higher courts? There seems to have been a downward trend in these even before 1968; but in the case of probation the fall – from 12·6 per cent to 8·7 per cent – was so sharp in 1968 that the suspended sentence probably contributed to it. On the other hand, one cannot be so sure in the case of discharges.

The Distributions of Prison Sentences

Table III of the *Criminal Statistics* shows the varying lengths of the prison sentences pronounced by Assizes and Quarter Sessions for different types of offence. This table poses several problems for those who wish to compare the lengths of sentences for different offences. A minor awkwardness is that it groups sentences of different lengths together, as follows:

'six months and under': most of these are of six months, but some are shorter;
'over six months and up to one year': although most of these are one-year sentences, a substantial minority are nine month terms;
'over one year and up to two years': these may be either eighteen month or two-year sentences;
and so on, although above two years sentences involving fractions of a year are rare. It would be more satisfactory to present the distribution as follows:

under six months
six months
intermediate
nine months
intermediate
one year

intermediate
eighteen months
intermediate
two years
and so on.

The main problem, however, arises when one wants to use the figures in order to make some fairly precise and yet concise statement about sentencing practice: for example when one wants to give some indication of the typical sentence for, say, burglary in a dwelling, and compare this with the typical sentence for robbery.

'Typical' is not, of course, a word with a precise scientific meaning. There are, however, some more precise concepts which might be employed.

The Mode

The mode is the easiest to use, since it is simply the value which occurs most often in a given sample. The *modal* length of sentence is the length which is pronounced more often than any other. Unfortunately the way in which Table III groups together sentences of nine and twelve months, sentences of eighteen and twenty-four months, and so on, makes it impossible to say with certainty which of these is the modal length. In any case, even if the subdivisions were improved, the modal length would still be a rather inadequate description of the sentencing pattern, as figures obtained from the Home Office show (see Table 9).

The table shows that there are really two very popular sentences for house breaking – twelve months and eighteen months. It would be misleading to describe twelve-month sentences as *the* mode simply because they exceeded the eighteen-month sentences by a margin of 0·2 per cent. The distribution is really *bi-modal*. Even so, sentences of nine months and twenty-four months are also popular.

The Mean

The mean (or 'average') is a concept familiar to most people. In this case it would be the sum of the lengths of all the sentences, divided by the number of sentences. Unfortunately, because of the subdivisions used in Table III, only a very approximate mean could be calculated from it. In any case, it is possible that very similar means could disguise very different distributions, as the example tabulated on page 54 shows.

Table 9

Prison* Sentences for House-Breaking† by Males, England and Wales, 1964–6

Nominal length‡ in months	% of all sentences
3 or less	2·3
4–6	9·9
7–9	13·4
10–12	19·0
13–15	4·7
16–18	18·8
19–21	1·6
22–4	12·6
25–30	2·6
31–6	9·2
37–48	3·0
49–60	1·9
61–72	0·1
73–84	0·4
85–96	0·4
97–108	—
109–20	0·1 (all 4 imposed in 1966)

All sentences; t otal: 5078=100·0

* Including corrective training and preventive detention, but not Borstal.

† Adult house-breakers are invariably sentenced at Assizes or Quarter Sessions, so that the limits which apply to magistrates' sentences have not affected the lengths of any of these sentences.

‡ Including the combined length of consecutive sentences. Of two or more concurrent sentences only the longest is counted. Remission is ignored.

The means are identical, but the distribution is very different. This is why statisticians, when giving averages, usually add a figure which indicates the amount of dispersion in the group, the measure most often used being the standard deviation (SD or σ). The standard deviations for group A and group B would be so different that they

Length in months	Group A Number of sentences	Group B Number of sentences
1	1	8
2	1	—
3	1	—
4	1	—
5	1	2
6	1	—
7	1	—
8	1	—
9	1	—
10	1	—
11	1	—
12	1	—
24	—	1
36	—	1
Mean length	6·5	6·5

would warn a statistician to look for marked differences in distribution in spite of the similarity of the averages.

Moreover, when the sample in question consists – as it does in the case of English prison sentences – of very large numbers clustering round the mean, there can be considerable fluctuations at the extremes of the distribution without an appreciable effect on the mean. Thus the higher courts might double or treble the tiny percentage of men on whom they imposed 'life' or sentences of more than ten years without altering the mean by more than a negligible fraction.

The Median

This is another useful measure. It is the point which separates the sentences into two halves. In Table 9 it seems to lie between the thirteen- to fifteen-month group and the sixteen- to eighteen-month group. Unfortunately it could happen that a sizeable group in the middle of the distribution made it impossible to split the sample into two equal, or even approximately equal, halves. Moreover, like the mean and the mode, the median gives no indication of the *spread* of the distribution.

It could be supplemented by indicating that, say, roughly half of the sentences which were below the median lay between it and ten months, while half of those above it lay between it and twenty-four months; but as Table 9 shows this would be only very roughly true, and when one tried to apply it to sentences for some other type of offence it might even be more inaccurate.

The Range

This is a term which is often used to describe sentencing patterns. Strictly speaking, it means the interval between the shortest and the longest sentence, and is usually described by giving their lengths. In the case of the sentences for house breaking set out in Table 9, the range is nearly ten years, i.e. from a month or two up to 120 months. Lawyers, however, tend to ignore the extremes of the range, and talk about 'the normal range' – a practice which can result in very imprecise statements. For example, in Table 9 it would be reasonable to exclude sentences over eight years on the grounds that they seem to occur only very occasionally (more precisely, not every year), and to talk of the normal range as being from under three months to ninety-six months. But lawyers go further than this, and use the term 'normal range' so as to exclude sentences of lengths which occur quite regularly, if not often, but which they regard in some way as exceptional, either because of their excessive length or because of their shortness. If they have grounds for doing so, this is not irrational. They may have good reason to say that a sentence of less than, say, nine months for house breaking must have been based on exceptional considerations. But the larger the percentages which they exclude in this way the more arbitrary and subjective their 'normal range' becomes. What is needed is some definition of the 'normal range' which can be applied in a non-arbitrary way to the distribution of sentence lengths for most types of offence.

One solution is to stipulate that the 'normal range' must not exclude more than, say, 20 per cent of the sentences, and that this 20 per cent must be evenly divided between the two extremes. (A range which thus excludes 10 per cent at each extreme is known as the 'decile' or 'inter-decile' range.) There is no special magic in the second of these stipulations. If one believed that very long sentences were more exceptional than very short ones (as seems to be the case) it would not be irrational to stipulate that the normal range should exclude 15 per cent at the higher extreme and 5 per cent at the lower extreme, *so long as this stipulation was applied uniformly to sentences for all types of offence which were being compared.* Unfortunately, the way in which sentence lengths are distributed makes it impossible to do even this in an exact way, as a glance at Table 9 shows. Any attempt to exclude stipulated percentages such as 5 per cent or 10 per cent at the extremes would have to be very approximate indeed.

In the circumstances, the best solution is probably to define the normal range as including the longest sentence which accounts for more than, say, 10 per cent of the sentences in question and the shortest sentence which does the same. Thus in Table 9 the normal range, so defined, would span all sentences from seven to nine months to twenty-two to twenty-four months, i.e. since sentences of seven, eight, twenty-two and twenty-three months are uncommon, from nine to twenty-four months. Again there is no special magic in the figure of 10 per cent: one could substitute 5 per cent or any percentage. Empirical research might one day establish that one or other percentage was most likely to discriminate between cases which sentencers regarded as 'exceptional' and those which they did not, but until it does all that can be offered is a common-sense convention of the kind suggested here.

Chapter 7
Custodial Statistics

Statistics relating to custodial institutions should not be overlooked by those who are interested in the penal system. The Home Office publishes an annual volume, *Report on the Work of the Prison Department: Statistical Tables,* which deals with prisons, Borstals and detention centres; it also compiles at intervals of six months unpublished tables relating to the populations of Borstals, detention centres and approved schools, which are available to libraries and research workers.

'Population' versus 'Receptions'

As always, it is important to be clear about what is being counted, and in particular to distinguish between 'population' and 'receptions' (sometimes called 'admissions', especially when hospitals are concerned). For example, very different pictures of the distribution of sentences of various lengths is given by a count of prison receptions and a count of the prison population, as can be seen from Table 10.

The percentages in brackets indicate the percentages of prisoners whose sentences are of the length shown *or less.* Thus the cumulative percentages for line 3 are the sums of the percentages for lines 1, 2 and 3; and they enable us to see that while only 45·8 of the male *population* of prisons in 1968 were serving sentences of eighteen months or less, no less than 84·2 of the men *received into* prison under sentence had been given such sentences.

It should not be concluded that one or other column is misleading. If we are planning prison accommodation and want to give better accommodation to long-sentence prisoners, clearly we should use the population column. If, on the other hand, we want a picture of the sentencing policy of the courts, the reception column is the appropriate

Table 10

Lengths of Sentences of Male Prisoners in 1968

Lengths*	Average population*		Receptions†	
	%	cumulative	%	cumulative
1. Up to 1 month	2·1	(2·1)	18·3	(18·3)
2. Over 1 and up to 6 months	15·5	(17·6)	40·5	(58·8)
3. Over 6 and up to 18 months	28·2	(45·8)	25·4	(84·2)
4. Over 18 months and under 3 years	18·1	(63·9)	7·8	(92·0)
5. 3 years	11·0	(74·9)	3·7	(95·7)
6. Over 3 and up to 10 years	21·6	(96·5)	4·0	(99·7)
7. Over 10 years (excluding life)	0·9	(97·4)	—	(99·7)
8. Life	2·6	(100·0)	0·3	(100·0)

* From Table E.2 in *Report on the Work of the Prison Department: Statistical Tables.*
† From Table C.5, ibid.

one. It must be realized, however, that both columns are based on *nominal* lengths of sentence (that is, those pronounced by the court) and do not reflect the time actually served, which is affected by remission and parole, and cannot be foreseen when prisoners are received. It would be possible in theory (although in practice the published figures do not do so) to show the times actually served by prisoners *released* each year: but if the policies of sentencers of the Parole Board were changing this would not be an accurate indication of the actual time likely to be served by prisoners entering prison in that year.

Actual Time Served

Nevertheless, a rough estimate of time actually served can be got by comparing the numbers of prisoners received under sentence (i.e. excluding those awaiting trial or sentence) with the average population (again excluding those awaiting trial or sentence). In 1968 the number of men *received* was 34,720 while the average male *population* was 20,965. Since more were received than were inside, the average length of time served must have been less than a year. More precisely, since the population represented about 60 per cent of the receptions, the mean time served must have been approximately 60 per cent of a year or seven months. A similar calculation for 1967 gives six months, however, and it seems that 1968 was an unusual year because of the introduction of the suspended sentence. A more reliable estimate would be based on several successive years' populations and receptions.

Failure to take into account the actual time spent 'inside' can lead to serious fallacies. For example, there has been concern over the numbers of suicides at remand centres (which receive men between their seventeenth and twenty-first birthdays while they are awaiting trial or sentence). If the suicide rate (e.g. suicides per 1000) for remand centre inmates is compared with the suicide rate for young males of roughly this age group, they are not too dissimilar, and one might be reassured. The comparison, however, is quite fallacious, because the suicide rate for young males in the general population is an *annual* rate, whereas the inmates of a remand centre spend only a small fraction of a year there. Let us suppose that their average stay lasts four weeks. If so, their suicide rate would have to be multiplied by thirteen to render it comparable with the incidence of suicides amongst young males over a period of fifty-two weeks.

Previous Penal Careers

There are other interesting tables in the *Report on the Work of the Prison Department: Statistical Tables.* One series (D.1–4) shows the previous proved offences and previous institutional sentences of persons sentenced to imprisonment for various types of offence, and makes it possible to calculate and compare the percentages of, say, adult males who are sentenced to imprisonment for their first offence, which can be used as a rough indication of the seriousness which courts attribute to different sorts of offence (see Table 11).

Although the offences which I have selected for inclusion in Table 11 were represented in fairly large numbers in the 1968 prison receptions, it would obviously be better still to base the percentages on figures for several successive years, in order to see whether the smaller differences – for example, between frauds and robberies – are due to mere sampling error.

Table 11

Percentages of Adult Males Sentenced to Imprisonment in 1968 without a Previous Proved Offence*

	%
Buggery and attempts, etc.	21·2
Sexual offences against females	21·4
Violence against the person other than murder	10·5
Frauds and false pretences	9·0
Robbery	7·0
Simple and minor larcenies	1·8
Breaking and entering	1·6
Taking motor vehicle without owner's consent	0·8
Malicious damage	0·7
Drunkenness	0·7
Indecent exposure	—
All offences	4·8

*The table does not make it clear whether previous non-indictable as well as indictable offences are counted.

Chapter 8
Measuring Trends

Criminal and judicial statistics are frequently studied in order to see whether changes are taking place: for example, whether violent crimes are increasing in frequency, or whether sentences are becoming more lenient.

Some of the problems involved in trying to answer questions of this kind have already been discussed, but the main pitfalls are listed here.

1. *Statistics of 'crimes made known to the police'*
(i) There may have been changes in the 'reportability' of the offences in question.
(ii) There may have been changes in police practice either as regards the acceptance of reports, or as regards the categories into which they are put.
(iii) There may have been changes in counting rules.
(iv) There may have been changes in the legal definitions of offences.
(v) Within whatever category of offence is being studied there may have been changes in the relative frequencies of different subdivisions (for example, murders for gain may become more or less frequent within a stable over-all murder rate).

2. *Statistics of crimes 'cleared-up'*
(i) There may have been changes in the definition of 'clearing up' (an example is the change of policy as regards crimes by under-age children, mentioned in Chapter 3, page 31).
(i) There may have been increases or decreases in types of offence which are virtually 'self-clearing-up'; that is, which point to the perpetrator as soon as they are reported (as incest does).

3. *Judicial statistics*
(i) There may have been changes in sentencers' powers (for example, restrictions on the use of imprisonment).

(ii) There may have been increases or decreases in the percentages of persons sentenced who have criminal records, or who ask for similar offences to be taken into consideration.

(iii) There may have been increases or decreases in what courts regard as more serious forms of the offence(s) in question.

(iv) There may have been changes in practice as regards the summary trial of indictable offences, so that more of a given type are dealt with by magistrates' courts instead of Quarter Sessions.

4. *Legislative and administrative delays*

(i) Not all legislation is brought into operation in the year in which it receives the Royal Assent. If the Act involves a good deal of administrative preparation, it is usual to enact that its provisions should come into operation only when an Order in Council is made to this effect. Nor are provisions always brought into operation at the beginning of a calendar year. Thus while the suspended sentence provisions of the Criminal Justice Act 1967 were brought into operation on 1 January 1968, the parole provisions, which entailed the review of several thousand prisoners already in prison, were not brought into effect until 1 April 1968.

(ii) Even after legislation has been brought into operation, it is not always fully effective at once, because of administrative difficulties. For example, the apparent caution with which courts began to make detention centre orders in 1952, and the slow increase in the number of such orders, is explained by the time which it took to provide detention centres; courts had to be content with a 'ration' of the available vacancies.

These are difficulties, however, which are peculiar to what is being counted. This chapter is mainly concerned with problems common to all or most types of criminal statistics and, of course, to other types of social statistics.

The Population at Risk

First, a question which should always be asked is 'What is the population at risk during the period in question?' If one is concerned with the distribution of different types of sentence the answer is obvious: the population at risk is the total of persons found guilty, or found guilty of a given offence, or found guilty of a given offence for the first time, and so on. Since the totals of persons found guilty are usually increasing, changes in sentencing policy are usually studied by expressing figures for persons fined, imprisoned and so on as percentages of these totals.

The population at risk is not quite so easy to define when one is concerned with trends in reported offences. It is common practice to express these as rates per 100,000 of the country's population. This is sometimes done, however, without considering what trend one is really interested in. Thus the question may be either 'Are potential victims of this offence more likely to become actual victims of it today than they were ten years ago?' or 'Are potential perpetrators of it more likely to become actual perpetrators than they were ten years ago?'

If the offence in question consists of indictable sexual interference with children, then the population of potential victims is restricted to children and young persons under sixteen, while the population of potential perpetrators consists of males (with negligible exceptions) nearly all of whom are at least ten years of age, and the great majority of whom are at least seventeen years of age. In other words, the incidence rate for such offences should be based on children under, say, sixteen if we want to compare probabilities of victimization, but on males aged ten or older if we want to know whether potential offenders are more likely to be actual offenders than they used to be.

Technical Aids

There are one or two simple devices which make it easier to interpret trends. One is the conversion of numbers – or of rates per head of population – to percentages of some selected figure. This is especially useful when one wants to answer questions which take the form 'Has x increased as much as y?', and when the numbers or rates involved are very different in scale. Thus McClintock and Avison, who wanted to compare the increases in recorded reports of different types of offence since the beginning of the century, took as their 'base' in each case the average annual numbers of reported offences of that type for the years 1901–1905, and represented the figures for selected subsequent years as percentages of these averages, with the result shown in Table 12. (A simpler base would have been the figures for 1901 alone; but they wanted to eliminate the possibility that a single year's figures might be atypical, as might well be the case for rare crimes such as murder.) It is not of course necessary to take the first year(s) of a series as the base, although this is usual because it makes for simplicity. For example, Figure 2, showing hospital orders and psychiatric probation orders, uses as a base the year 1961, because this was the first complete year in which hospital orders could be made under the Mental Health Act 1959: but it was not the first year in which psychiatric probation orders could be made.

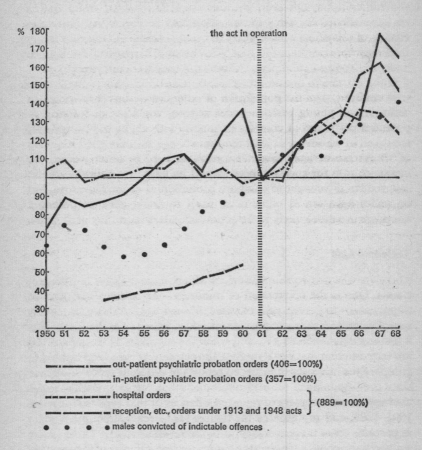

Figure 2 The effects of the Mental Health Act 1959

64 Measuring Trends

Table 12

Rates of Change for Different Classes of Offences in Selected Years from 1901–1963

Classification of offences according to relative magnitude of percentages increase between 1901–1905 and 1963.	Rate of change: annual average $1901–1905 = 100$				
Annual average 1901–1905 = 100	1921	1938	1948	1961	1963
1. High increase (> 1700)					
Malicious woundings	56	174	386	1520	1779
Homosexual offences	178	572	1405	2513	2437
Shopbreaking	206	556	1464	1990	2568
Attempted breakings	218	1088	2392	3213	4186
Larceny from dwelling house	140	767	2428	3068	3903
Forgery	138	396	1449	1688	2106
2. Medium high increase (1300 < 1700)					
Housebreaking	141	377	710	1051	1427
Receiving	160	295	777	1184	1527
Malicious damage	108	113	737	1110	1373
3. Average increase (900 < 1300)					
Heterosexual offences	155	282	588	1218	1248
Robbery	86	117	449	959	1013
Simple and minor larcenies	115	335	557	879	1053
Frauds and false pretences	187	420	506	1042	1204
4. Low increase (< 500) or decrease					
Murder	88	74	110	94	98
Felonious woundings, etc.	84	127	194	440	450
Larceny by servant and embezzlement	90	141	281	331	360
Larceny from the person	46	61	121	136	146
Total indictable crimes	118	323	597	921	1117
Males in the home population aged 15–49	115	130	135	131	130

Source: McClintock and Avison (1968, p. 30). The figures for males in the population aged 15–49, however, have been added to illustrate the point made in the text.

Moving Averages

Another device, the moving average, is useful when one is trying to discern trends in numbers which are small enough to be affected by chance annual fluctuations. Since these fluctuations make it difficult to follow any long-term trend, it is useful to be able to smooth them out. One way of doing so is to replace each annual figure by an average of the figures for two or more consecutive years which include that year. For example, the annual numbers of persons found unfit to plead at their trial are small, and therefore subject to marked fluctuations which disguise long-term trends, as Table 13 shows.

Table 13

Persons for Trial and Found Unfit to Plead

Year	Persons for trial	Persons found unfit to plead
1946	17,682	25
1947	20,142	34
1948	22,931	48
1949	19,476	38
1950	18,858	36
1951	19,934	25
1952	22,070	25
1953	20,197	31
1954	18,676	39
1955	18,012	31
1956	19,493	35
1957	22,861	35
1958	27,740	40
1959	29,527	51
1960	30,505	30
1961	34,236	36
1962	32,943	25
1963	25,529	25
1964	24,209	23
1965	26,783	26

Source: Criminal Statistics.

The trend becomes much clearer if three operations are performed on the figures. First, they should be expressed as rates per 100,000 persons at risk, which in this case means persons brought to trial (*not* persons found guilty, or persons tried, since a finding of unfitness to plead usually takes place before the trial begins). Second, minor fluctuations should be smoothed out by converting the annual rates to three-year moving averages (for example, by converting the figure for 1947 to the average for 1946, 1947 and 1948, and the figure for 1948 to the average for 1947–9). Third, the three-year moving average can be drawn as a graph. It then becomes clear that there has been a downward trend since the Second World War, interrupted by a small upsurge in 1953–5.

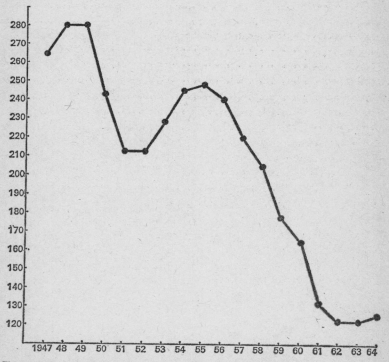

Figure 3 Persons found unfit for trial from 1947 to 1964 shown as three-year moving average rates per 100,000 persons for trial (from Walker, 1968, p. 233)

A cruder but less laborious method is simply to average the figures for groups of successive years, as is done for certain quinquennia in Table A of the *Criminal Statistics*. So far as the measurement of long-term changes are concerned this is not unsatisfactory. But it may, of course, conceal short-term changes. In the example just given, the short-lived upsurge of cases of unfitness to plead in the middle of the 1950s would have been obliterated if the rates had been expressed simply as averages for the quinquennia 1950–54, 1955–9 and 1960–64.

Chapter 9
Indexing Crime

An important problem in the counting of offences arises from the fact that they are so varied in nature. Some result in death or serious injury to people, others cause sexual harm, others inflict losses of property on individuals or on large corporations, others merely inconvenience people. Sometimes the harm is actually done; in other cases it is averted through pure chance or the incompetence of the offender. Some offences, as we have seen, involve whole series of acts or omissions, spread over days, weeks or months: others are momentary. Yet the usual way of comparing one year's crimes, or one area's crimes, with another is simply to count them in the same way as houses or books are counted: that is, by disregarding differences in shape, size, material or contents.

This could be extremely misleading. Suppose that we are told simply that in one year (or one area) a thousand offences were committed whereas in another only 900 were. This crude comparison might conceal the fact that the lower figure included more murders than the higher figure, but fewer parking offences.

This danger is to some extent reduced by distinguishing between the offences which are, by official agreement at least, considered serious and those which are not. In England it is usual to distinguish indictable and non-indictable offences, motoring and non-motoring offences, when making comparisons between different years or police districts. But 'indictable offences' mean everything from murder to the theft of a box of matches from a shop. So the *Criminal Statistics* subdivide them, in the graphs for post-war years, into 'larceny', 'breaking and entering', 'receiving, frauds and false pretences', 'sexual offences' and 'violence against the person'. This is better still; the more of these common-sense subdivisions there are, the more homogeneous the offences which they comprise. We can see from the graphs in the *Criminal Statistics* that since 1950 (*a*) there has been a steady rise in personal violence, but that it is still far less common than the other sorts of recorded offences; (*b*) sexual offences rose in the 1950s, but seemed to remain fairly steady in numbers during the 1960s; (*c*) property offences rose in the early 1950s, fell in the middle 1950s, and have been rising ever since.

Even this is not entirely satisfactory. 'Sexual offences', for example, include such diverse behaviour as rape, buggery, intercourse with under-age girls and incest (but exclude, in this case, indecent exposure and soliciting, since these are non-indictable). A glance at Table A of the *Criminal Statistics* shows that rapes and indecent assaults on women – or more precisely reports of these – have in fact been increasing, while reported homosexual offences have been decreasing, probably for the reasons explained in Chapter 1.

Is the solution further subdivisions? This would certainly increase the accuracy of comparisons. But another approach has been suggested: the 'weighted index'. Essentially, this assumes that it is reasonable to add up even quite dissimilar offences provided that a system of 'weighting' is used. 'Weighting' means assigning different values to different offences instead of merely counting them: for example, counting 10 for each murder, 9 for each serious assault or act of sexual molestation, 5 for a robbery, 1 for a theft, and so on. This makes it possible to arrive at what is called an index of crime which takes account of the greater seriousness of certain offences.

So far so good: but how are we supposed to arrive at our system of weighting? How do we know whether to give robbery ten or twenty or a hundred times as many points as theft? There is no solution which is both objective and satisfactory. At first sight it would be objective to assign weights according to the frequency of the offence, inverting the relationship so that the rarer it was the more it would score. This would give murder, rape and espionage very high scores, and theft a low score, which would probably accord with most people's notions of relative seriousness. There would be awkward exceptions, however: recorded bigamy is as rare as murder nowadays, but nobody takes it as seriously. Moreover, this system of weighting would be only apparently based on objective frequencies, for it would be strongly affected by the reportability of different offences.

A solution which has been put forward in the past is to base the weighting on the sentences for different types of offence – either on the maximum permissible sentences or on the actual sentences (for example, on the percentage of offenders sent to prison, or sent to prison for more than six months). In either form this would be most unsatisfactory. Nobody seriously defends the rationality of the maxima for offences in English statutes (which for example allow courts to impose ten years for theft but only two years for cruelty to a child). Actual sentences would be somewhat less unsatisfactory. It is true that they would simply be an indirect way of asking judges, recorders and magistrates for their views on the relative seriousness of offences; but one could do worse, as we shall see. Judges, magistrates and recorders pass sentence after hearing details of each offender, and are thus to some extent assessing its seriousness from the facts. The difficulty is that they are also influenced by information about the offender which, though relevant from the sentencing point of view, may be quite irrelevant to the seriousness of the offence. For example, we saw in Chapter 6 that shopbreakers appeared to be sentenced more heavily than men of violence, but probably because they had longer records.

This difficulty might be to some extent overcome by using only sentences imposed on first offenders as a basis for weighting (for example, Table 11 in Chapter 7 shows how the percentage of 'first offenders' varies amongst men imprisoned for different types of crime in a way which seems to reflect the 'seriousness' of the different types in the eyes of the court). Even this expedient, however, could not exclude the effect on the sentencer of mitigating or aggravating circumstances, although it could perhaps be assumed that these would be distributed randomly amongst the different sorts of crime.

The Sellin–Wolfgang Method

The solution adopted by Sellin and Wolfgang (1964) was to devise a system of weighting by describing 141 carefully prepared accounts of different crimes to three samples of people – policemen, university students and juvenile court judges. The accounts of the different crimes were varied so as to include, in various combinations, 'elements' such as the death or hospitalization of the victim, the use of a weapon, forcible entry of premises and the value of property stolen, damaged or destroyed. For example:

The offender robs a person at gunpoint. The victim struggles and is shot to death.
The offender forces open a cash register in a department store and steals five dollars.
The offender smokes marihuana.

Members of the samples were asked to rate each of these on a scale,[1] and their ratings were used to construct the weighting system. In this, for example, a crime with the following 'elements' would be given the number of points shown:

A house is forcibly entered	1
a man is murdered	26
his wife receiving minor injury	1
and between 251 and 2000 dollars taken.	2
Total score	30

It is possible to criticize Sellin and Wolfgang's techniques[2] as well as their choice of groups to sample. The central question, however, is not whether their approach could be improved but whether it really is profitable. What is it intended to do, and does it succeed in doing it? The authors summarize its purpose in their admirably clear little manual (*Constructing an Index of Delinquency*, 1963):

The need for an index. In most communities . . . the problem of delinquency is of growing concern. Many proposals for dealing with it have been and are advanced in the hope that if they are materialized delinquency will be curbed or reduced, and many of them are actually in operation in many communities. In order to evaluate their effectiveness, however, it is necessary to determine the character and trend of delinquency. To do so requires more sensitive measuring devices than those now available. It is the purpose of this Manual to indicate how such an instrument may be constructed and used.

1. For reasons explained in chapter 15 of *The Measurement of Delinquency*, the authors used two scales, a 'category scale' and a 'magnitude estimating scale'; but the refinements of their technique are not under discussion here.
2. See, for example, the article by Rose (1966) and the reply by Ackman, Figlio and Normandeau (1967).

What seems to be intended is that for different communities and for different dates an index of reported offences should be compiled. Thus the index for Sodom in 1970 might be 117,634 while for Gomorrah it might be 219,835; and for the same towns in 1975 it might be 128,001 and 213,111 respectively. What is not made clear is in what way this would be an improvement on the crude system of counting each reported crime as one. It might appear to tell us that Gomorrah had a more serious crime problem than Sodom (assuming the two towns to be of comparable size[3]), but it would not tell us whether this was because Gomorrah's crimes included more murders, personal violence and the use of weapons, or because it included a very large number of lucrative thefts, burglaries and frauds. In other words it would be *less* informative than a small table of the following kind, which would, incidentally, be less laborious to compile:

Type of offence	Sodom	Gomorrah
Violence causing death or hospitalization in course of acquisitive crime	36	145
Other violence	178	202
Breakings and enterings without personal violence	989	1001
Thefts, frauds, etc.	7888	10,243
Sexual offences against women	222	142
Sexual offences against children	665	20

This would give a much clearer picture of the differences between the patterns of crime in the two towns.

'Criminotypes'

An index which is in effect a shorthand method of conveying information of this sort was suggested by McClintock and Avison (1968, ch. 3). Their method, which they called 'criminotyping', was as follows:

1. They worked out, for each of the 125 police areas in the country,

3. Presumably these figures could also be represented as rates per head of population if one wanted to compare the relative wickedness of two towns of different size.

the rates per 100,000 of the population for four groups of offence: violent and sexual offences together, breaking and entering offences, larceny and a combination of what they called 'selected serious crimes' (which included some of the other groups).

2. Using the rates for each of these four offence groups in turn, they ranked their 125 police areas in order, so that the one with the lowest rate was at the top and the one with the highest at the bottom of the list.

3. They then divided the list into nine groups, each containing fourteen police areas (although one group, the middle one, had to be one short), and numbered each group from one (the group with the lowest rates) to nine (with the highest).

Thus each police area was given four numbers, each indicating how high it ranked so far as rates for one of the offence groups were concerned. The composite group was placed last, and separated from the others by an oblique stroke.

The area with the worst ranking for 1965 was Nottingham, with 999/9: it was thus in the worst group for all four offence-types. The best was Mid-Wales, with 111/1. An intermediate area was Dorset, with 436/5.

It would be possible to criticize McClintock and Avison on points of secondary importance, such as the lumping together of violent and sexual crimes. Nevertheless their method is in principle greatly preferable to that of Sellin and Wolfgang's, both for its simplicity and for its informativeness. It is true that unlike the Sellin–Wolfgang index it cannot be used to tell us whether the entire country's crimes are growing more or less serious, for it depends on ranking subdivisions of the country. It is doubtful, however, whether the Sellin–Wolfgang index is a desirable way of measuring changes in crime over time, again because the method of compilation could well conceal marked changes in the pattern of crime between one year and another.

The Perks Committee rightly rejected the idea of an over-all index of the Sellin–Wolfgang type, although the only reason given for doing so was that 'any weights that could be assigned would necessarily be controversial'. They preferred the use of several 'indicators': for example, a 'homicide indicator' which would include both murder and attempted murder. Where an offence group included offences differing widely in seriousness, they suggested selecting one or two of the more serious subdivisions, and simply leaving the rest out of the 'indicator'. They did not wholly oppose the idea of 'weighting', which they thought might be suitable for property offences, for which the value of goods stolen or damaged could be used. On the whole, however, they were not enthusiastic about weighting, and rightly so.

Why Index At All?

A question which seems central to the whole problem, but which does not seem to have been discussed by any of the proponents of an index, is 'What useful task would it perform that could not be performed by simple counting subdivisions of crime or selected crimes?' The answer cannot be that it would convey more information. The McClintock–Avison 'criminotype' is a neat and fairly objective shorthand method of comparing areas' reported crime-rates for selected subdivisions of crime; but it does not deepen our knowledge beyond that. The Sellin–Wolfgang index seems almost designed to conceal differences in the pattern of crime.

It might be argued, however, that such indices are useful for decision-making. If so, what sorts of decisions? Certainly if I were choosing an area for my retirement I might use the McClintock–Avison criminotype, which would tell me that I and my family would be safer in Mid-Wales than in Oxford. But would either form of index help law-enforcement agencies in their decision-making? Would it, for example, help in deciding whether one city needed more police than another? It might; but this could be done better by an index based on the fact that some types of crime make more demands on police man-hours than others. This illustrates the advisability of considering what sort of decision-making the index is meant to assist, before working out the method of constructing it. Otherwise one may end with an index which merely tells us whether we should be more worried about crime in 1970 (or in Wigan) than we were (or should have been) in 1969 (or Weston-super-Mare): a boon to writers of editorials, but little more.

Chapter 10
Measuring Association

The assessment of numerical evidence for associations between variables is a subject which is usually left to textbooks on statistics, and with some justice, since it can call for a considerable degree of technical expertise. Nevertheless there are several points which can be made even in this context.

Measurement of association is the tool most frequently used by social scientists in searching for or testing the existence of causal links between phenomena. In order to do this they must be able to simplify situations by minimizing the effect of irrelevant variables, that is, variables other than those in which they are interested at the moment. This they do either by setting up an experimental situation, or by selecting events from life in such a way as to minimize the effect of the irrelevant variables.

An Experimental Situation

A simple example of an experiment is provided by Rita Simon (1967). Sixty-eight 'juries', selected by ballot from real jury 'pools' in Chicago, St Louis and Minneapolis, listened to a tape-recorded version of the trial of a man for incest. His defence was insanity, and at the end of the trial twenty of the 'juries' heard a 'judge' instruct them as to the test which they should apply to this defence under the M'Naghten Rules. Another twenty-six 'juries' received a different sort of judicial instruction, based on the Durham Rule, which has been substituted for the M'Naghten Rules in some jurisdictions of the USA.[1] The remaining

1. In this experiment the essences of the different Rules were expressed as follows (see Simon, 1967, p. 45):
M'Naghten: the defendant must have been 'incapable of understanding the nature, quality and consequences of his acts, or of distinguishing between right and wrong'.
Durham: the defendant's act must have 'stemmed from and been the product of mental disease or defect'.

group of twenty-two 'juries' received no instruction on the subject. Their verdicts were:

	Defence succeeded	Jury 'hung'	Defence failed	Total
'M'Naghten juries'	0	1	19	20
'Durham juries'	5	6	15	26
Uninstructed juries	4	4	14	22

By ensuring that each 'jury' listened to the same 'trial', in which only one variable – the 'judge's' instruction – was varied, Miss Simon did her best to produce an experimental situation. There was of course the possibility that irrelevant variables would intervene in the jury-room: for example, that the 'M'Naghten juries' contained, by chance, some influential jurors who were particularly unsympathetic to psychiatric evidence. As a precaution, however, Miss Simon had asked each juror for his own individual verdict before he took part in the discussions leading to a 'verdict', and the pattern was the same as that of the groups' verdicts. Those who had been instructed on M'Naghten lines were much less likely to accept the insanity defence than those who were either uninstructed or instructed on Durham lines; and the last two groups were very similar in their distribution. The figures suggest that the M'Naghten Rule is much more likely than the Durham Rule to lead to a rejection of the insanity defence, and that the effect of the Durham Rule is not very different from leaving the test to the jury to work out for themselves.[2]

Scientific Selection

Suppose, however, that Miss Simon had been unable, for some reason, to set up an experimental situation of this kind. She would have had to do what other social scientists are often forced to do: proceed by scientific selection instead of experiment. She would have had to take samples of actual trials in which the M'Naghten Rule and the Durham Rule were used in instructing jurors.[3] She would then have had to

2. She might well have been unable to find trials in which the insanity defence was offered without any judicial instruction to jurors on the Rule to apply.

3. But see Chapter 11 on the significance of numerical differences between samples.

consider the irrelevant variables which might interfere. For example, the M'Naghten juries might be trying cases in which the nature of the charges was likely to prejudice them against the defendant. Or they might have heard psychiatric evidence which was unconvincingly handled or skilfully attacked on cross-examination. The larger the numbers in each sample the less likely would it be that chance differences of this kind would distinguish them; but it is not easy to collect large samples of insanity defences, even in the USA, and even less easy to collect samples of the Durham Rule in use. Miss Simon would, therefore, have had to try to 'match' her sample, for example, by ensuring that murder trials were not more frequent in the M'Naghten sample than in the Durham sample.

In this way it is just conceivable that she might have rendered her samples sufficiently comparable to feel justified in treating their verdicts as tests of the effect of the two Rules. (The question 'How large would the difference between the percentages of "guilty" verdicts have to be before she could safely base inferences on it?' is discussed in Chapter 11.)

A simple example of an actual attempt to use scientific selection instead of experimental control is also concerned with the behaviour of juries. Kalven and Zeisel, who were able to collect data about some 3500 real jury trials, wanted to answer, *inter alia*, the question 'Other things being equal, have women a better chance of acquittal than men?' Unfortunately, as they realized, women's crimes tend on the whole to be very different from men's, so that a crude comparison of acquittal rates would have been misleading. They were able, however, to select seventeen trials of women for the murder of their husbands, and compare them with twenty-seven trials of men for the murder of their wives, with the following result:

	Where defendant was	
	wife	*husband*
	%	%
Jury convicted	59	82
Jury 'hung'	—	11
Jury acquitted	41	7
	100	100

Since the person responsible for the killing is hardly ever in doubt in such cases, acquittal depends on the jury's sympathy with defences such as provocation, self-defence, accident and insanity. Although the matching could be criticized as too simple, the example is a neat illustration of ingenious selection.

How could the matching have been improved? By taking variables which were known to affect the jury's sympathy with the defendant, such as being coloured, or being elderly, and ensuring that both the husbands and the wives included equal percentages of coloured and elderly individuals. This could be done in two ways: group matching and one-to-one matching. In group matching one is content if the percentages for each variable are roughly the same, while in one-to-one matching one tries to pair members of the two samples so that members of each pair correspond as regards each of the variables: in this case so that for each coloured elderly female defendant there is a coloured elderly male defendant, for each young white female defendant there is a young white male defendant, and so on. One-to-one matching, though more difficult to achieve, is more rigorous and satisfactory than group matching. For in the example we are considering we could ensure by group matching that, say, one third of each sample was coloured, and one quarter elderly: but this would not ensure that the two samples contain equal percentages of coloured elderly people, and the combination might be causally important.

Visual Aids to Interpretation

The examples we have been considering were chosen because of their simplicity. The relevant variables either were or could be treated as qualitative, which by their nature divided themselves into obvious categories. Juries can do only three things – accept the defence, reject it or fail to reach any verdict. The instruction to the jury must either be silent on the subject of the insanity defence, or take one of the approved forms.[4] Consequently, the tabulation of the results is easy, and the table simple to interpret. Often, however, the available data are more complex. They may be quantitative instead of qualitative. Instead of two or three situations there may be dozens. An example

4. Although we must not completely discount the occurrence of minor variations in wording which *may* have an effect.

can be found in Table V of the *Criminal Statistics* (see pages 152–3) which deals with appeals against conviction and sentence by higher courts. If the percentage of offenders who appeal against sentence is calculated from that table and from Table IIa (see pages 150–51), it can be seen to vary considerably for different offences. Column (*a*) of Table 14 below, which is based on the 1967 figures, shows the appeal rate for offence groups which are represented in sufficient numbers in Table V. What is likely to be responsible for these differences? Two obvious possibilities can be tested: one is the appellants' estimates of their chances of success, the other is the nature of their sentences. Columns (*b*) and (*c*) of Table 14, therefore, show the success rates of appeals against sentence[5] and the percentage of custodial sentences for these offences in 1967.

Table 14

Offence group	(a) Appeal rate (against sentence or sentence and conviction) %	(b) Success rate of such appeals in 1965+1966 %	(c) Prison sentences as % of all sentences in 1967	(d) Prison sentences exceeding 6 months as % of all sentences in 1967
Wounding (felony)	22·2	5·4	75·4	59·0
Wounding (misdemeanor)	19·3	3·2	54·7	32·9
Buggery, etc.	11·0	6·3	31·7	14·7
Rape	32·5	1·4	88·3	69·0
Breaking and entering	12·3	5·4	61·5	34·9
Robbery	27·1	3·8	83·0	53·2
Larceny	23·5	5·8	55·8	43·8
Fraud	20·2	13·8	38·5	35·5
Receiving	18·9	10·0	51·4	40·2
Motoring offence	6·4	5·6	15·0	6·2

It is fairly obvious from a mere inspection of columns (*a*) and (*b*) that there is little relationship between them. It is true that the low

5. Based on the two preceding years, since appellants could not be aware of the current year's success rate.

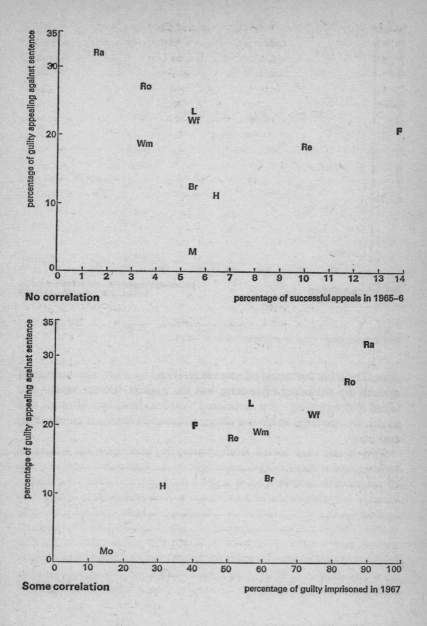

No correlation

percentage of successful appeals in 1965–6

Some correlation

percentage of guilty imprisoned in 1967

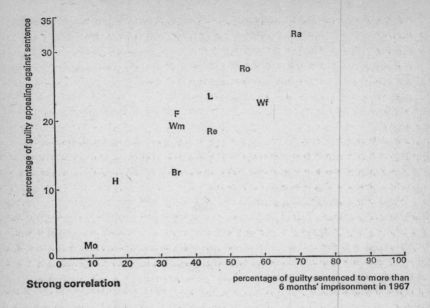

Strong correlation

percentage of guilty sentenced to more than 6 months' imprisonment in 1967

Figure 4 The association between appeal rates, appeal success rates and prison sentences (for higher courts only)

appeal rate for motoring offences is matched by a low success rate of appeals by motoring offenders; but the highest success rates – for fraud and receiving – are associated with middling appeal rates; and so on. But perhaps there is a closer association between columns (a) and (c)?

This is not easy to tell from inspection, and there are statistical techniques for measuring the strength of the association between sets of values such as this. This is a good example, however, of a case in which a very simple use of a visual aid will be sufficient, in spite of the fact that it cannot quantify the strength of the association in the way in which statistical techniques could do. The visual aid in this case is a scatter-diagram (see Figure 4) in which the percentages in column (a) are plotted along one coordinate and the percentages in column (c) along the other. If the association were a very close one, the different offence groups would be arranged in a line, which might be

82 Measuring Association

straight or curved but would rise from somewhere in the bottom left corner towards the top right corner. The scatter-diagram for columns (a) and (c) does not achieve so neat a pattern, but the offence groups show a tendency to range from bottom left to top right. Clearly there is some causal relationship at work. But perhaps what really prompts an appeal is not so much a prison sentence as a prison sentence of substantial length? This can be tested by consulting Table III of the *Criminal Statistics*, which subdivides prison sentences according to their lengths. Prison sentences of, say, more than six months can be expressed as percentages of all sentences for each offence group, as is done in column (d) of Table 14.

If we now draw a scatter-diagram from the percentages in columns (a) and (d), the result is a very definite pattern, in which the offence groups are arranged in a narrow band from bottom left to top right. Clearly the appeal rate is more closely associated with the frequency of substantial prison sentences than with the variables in columns (b) or (c). It is possible to carry the process further, since Table III of the *Criminal Statistics* makes it possible to calculate similar percentages for prison sentences exceeding one, two, three years and so on; readers can draw their own scatter-diagrams and see for themselves whether the association would have been closer if column (d) had been based on sentences of some greater length.

Correlations over Time

A slightly different problem arises when one wants to study the relationship between variables which vary over a period of time. A good example is provided by Wilkins (1964, pp. 54–5). Wilkins wondered how closely the frequency of thefts from unattended cars and lorries depended on the *opportunities* for this sort of stealing. As a rough index of 'opportunities' he was able to use the numbers of private motor vehicles registered: the two sets of figures are set out in Table 15.

Here again there are techniques for quantifying the degree of association between the two variables. But Wilkins, although a sophisticated statistician, employed the simple device of the graph, plotting both variables along the same time-scale. He had one difficulty to overcome: that the numbers for one variable were enormously greater than the numbers for the other. His solution again was a simple

Table 15

**The number of (*a*) Private Motor Vehicles Registered and
(*b*) Cases of Larceny from Motor Vehicles (Known to the Police)**

Year	(*a*) Motor vehicles	(*b*) Larceny from motor vehicles
1938	1,944,000	25,281
1940	1,423,000	16,849
1941	1,503,000	15,672
1942	858,000	12,180
1943	718,000	11,084
1944	755,000	14,509
1945	1,487,000	26,520
1946	1,770,000	32,546
1947	1,943,000	33,984
1948	1,961,000	32,665
1949	2,131,000	30,297
1950	2,258,000	33,156
1951	2,380,000	43,127
1952	2,508,000	41,125
1953	2,762,000	39,739
1954	3,100,000	39,398
1955	3,526,000	43,304
1956	3,888,000	50,782
1957	4,187,000	54,937
1958	4,549,000	68,466
1959	4,966,000	79,899
1960	5,526,000	92,704
1961	5,979,000	112,671

one: to calculate the mean (average) number for each variable over
the whole period, and to represent the annual values as percentages of
the mean. The result was Figure 5, which demonstrates a very close
relationship between opportunity for, and frequency of, this type of
crime. As a precaution, he also tabulated the numbers of one other
type of crime – known larcenies from shops and stalls – to see whether
these fluctuated in the same way. If they had, this would have cast
doubt on the causal relationship between numbers of vehicles and
thefts from them, but fortunately they did not.

84   Measuring Association

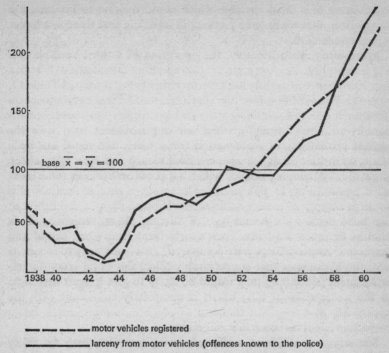

- - - - - motor vehicles registered
——————— larceny from motor vehicles (offences known to the police)

Figure 5 The relationship between opportunities to commit crime and the incidence of crime (from Wilkins, 1964, p. 54)

Complications

Most of the examples discussed in these notes have been chosen so as to avoid raising an awkward question, 'Can the study of associations in these ways point infallibly to causal relationships?' The answer is 'Only in special circumstances'. There is nearly always the possibility that A is associated with X because some third variable, which has not been tabulated, is causing the variations in both. In an experimental situation, such as Miss Simon's 'trials', this possibility can usually be reduced to negligible size. In the case of data selected from real life – of which the appeals against sentence are an example – a direct causal connection between the two tabulated variables may be so obviously in accordance with common sense, or it may be so difficult

Complications 85

to conceive of a third variable which could operate to produce the association, that we may be justified in inferring that there is a direct causal connection.

More often, unfortunately, the operation of a third variable is a real possibility. An example is the apparent association between imprisonment and unduly high reconviction rates, shown in Table 17, page 115. One cannot safely infer that imprisonment *raises* reconviction rates until one has eliminated the real possibility that courts intentionally or unintentionally select for imprisonment men with the highest probability of reconviction (even when allowance has been made, as in that table, for age, criminal record and type of offence). Occasionally there is evidence which supports or weakens these awkward possibilities. In this case, for example, a similar analysis of a Scottish sample of male first offenders showed that, after allowance had been made for age and type of offence, prison sentences of six months or more did better than shorter sentences when actual and 'expected' reconvictions were compared. This is not easy to reconcile with the hypothesis that courts simply select the worst risks for imprisonment (since if so they would be likely to give longest sentences to the worst risks of all); but it is completely consistent with the hypothesis that a prison sentence of some minimum length has a corrective effect on some first offenders.

Sometimes a different awkwardness arises. One may be fairly confident that there is a direct causal link between two variables, but be uncertain which is cause and which effect. In the examples of the insanity defence experiment and the appeal rate table the direction of causation was beyond doubt, because the 'judge's' instructions and the sentences of imprisonment had been uttered before the 'juries'' verdicts or the prisoners' appeals, as the case may be. But suppose that one finds, as R. G. Andry did (1960) that delinquency in boys is associated with poor relationships with their fathers. Even if one can disregard the possibility of a third causal variable, can one be sure that it is the paternal relationship which is the 'independent variable', i.e. causes the delinquency? May not the delinquency have impaired the relationship? As it happens, there is an American study in which boys whose relationships with their fathers were bad were found to be more likely to become delinquent *later*; see McCord and McCord (1959).

86 Measuring Association

Chapter 11
Significance

A problem which arises sooner or later in the comparison of samples which are assumed to be comparable is the 'significance' to be attached to differences. Are they differences which could have arisen by chance, or can they safely be regarded as indicating that there is a real difference of some sort between the two samples? I say 'samples' because it is very difficult to think of any sort of criminal statistics which, for inferential purposes, is not a sample, that is, a selection from a larger 'population'. For inferential purposes even the total of one and a half million appearances in English and Welsh criminal courts which led to convictions in 1968 is a sample of such appearances in the late 1960s, unless one simply wishes to confine one's statements and inferences to the year 1968.

Careful selection of a sample will eliminate obvious kinds of bias and, of course, the larger the sampling fraction the more representative it is likely to be of its population: a 50 per cent sample is more likely to be representative than a 10 per cent sample, given the same precautions. No amount of care in sampling, however, can eliminate the possibility that two or more samples taken from the same population will differ slightly in regard to the variables in which one is interested. What one wants to know when one finds differences is the probability that they are simply due to sampling error of this kind. If this probability is high, one is not justified in basing inferences on them. But if it is low, then it is reasonable to assume that the samples are from populations which differ in the same way, and one can proceed to inferences. Loosely speaking, therefore, the 'significance' of numerical differences is the probability that they are due to something more than mere sampling error.

Suppose for example that we want to answer the question 'Is the Court of Appeal more likely to interfere with a conviction or with a sentence?' and all we have is a sample consisting of appeals heard in 1968. Columns 14 to 19 of Table V of the *Criminal Statistics* for that year show that of 248 (150+7+91) appeals against conviction which were actually heard, 150 (60 per cent) were unsuccessful, whereas of 577 (212+315+50) appeals against sentence which were heard, 212 (37 per cent) were unsuccessful. How reliable is the inference that an appeal against sentence is more likely to succeed? In more precise terms, what is the probability that the difference between 37 per cent and 60 per cent is due to nothing more than sampling error? This probability can be calculated, and is a good deal less than one in a thousand: in statistical terms this would be stated in the form '$p < 0.001$'. In other words, one could say with some confidence that there is some factor which gives appeals against sentence a bigger chance of success; and if one is able to look at the corresponding tables for other years one finds that the difference is in fact in the same direction, although the actual percentages are different.

In contrast, consider the question 'Is a sentence for robbery more likely to be varied by the Court of Appeal than one for an offence of breaking and entering?' The figures for 1968 (offence groups 27 to 33 and 34) are as follows: 27 out of 48 sentences for robbery (56 per cent) were varied, as compared with 85 out of 133 for breaking and entering (65 per cent). In this case, both the numbers involved and the gap between the percentages are smaller, and in consequence 'p' is larger: it is greater than one in ten. So it would be risky to infer that there is something about sentences for robbery which makes them less likely to be varied, although by adding up the figures for previous years, which point in the same direction, 'p' can be reduced and one's confidence in the inference increased.

Levels of Significance

The verdicts of Rita Simon's juries, however, fell into an intermediate category. She noted that the difference between the verdicts of her M'Naghten and her Durham juries had a probability of being due to sampling error that was less than 0.05 (and the same was true of the difference between the M'Naghten juries and the uninstructed juries). This is a level of significance which social scientists regard as insufficient for really confident inference, but sufficient to justify discussion and further investigation. There is no natural dividing point between values of p which are accepted as bases for inference and those which are not. The 0·05 level seems simply to have been adopted by a convention as the point beyond which one does not take results very seriously, just as the 0·01 level has been adopted as the point at which one is allowed to talk as if one's results could not be due to mere sampling error.

The calculation of significance can be learned from elementary textbooks of statistics (e.g. Conway, 1967, ch. 12). In some cases, however, it is possible to make use of a very easy visual aid called a nomograph, which will be found in Oppenheim (1966, Appendix 3). This demands only a transparent ruler and an ability to calculate percentages; and even the latter can be replaced by a slide-rule. Whatever test one is using, however, it is advisable to ask a statistician to confirm that it is appropriate to the problem in question.

One simple danger, however, must be appreciated. Some investigations involve the study of such large numbers of apparent associations between variables that some of these associations may well pass the test of significance by pure chance. If one compiles 200 tables, and finds that, say, forty of them show an association which is significant at the 0·05 level (i.e. the one in twenty level), then about two out of the forty (i.e. one in twenty) are likely to have passed this test by chance. Sometimes it is possible to say that all (or most) of the tables present a consistent picture or, on the other hand, that one or more of the associations seems obviously unlikely in view of the picture presented by the others. But if common sense will not help, one must just raise one's required level of significance; and in such cases 0·05 sets too low a standard.

Chapter 12
Measuring Deterrent Efficacy

Whether one is a judge, recorder, magistrate, probation officer or penal administrator, a question which one must face is 'What do we know about the efficacy of the different choices open to sentencers, and of different methods of giving effect to choices such as probation or imprisonment?' Unless one is prepared to accept someone else's answers uncritically, one must understand the logic and a little of the arithmetic involved in scientific attempts to measure penal efficacy.

The difficulty of the problem varies with the object of the sentence. If this is retributive – that is, to impose suffering, hardship or inconvenience proportionate to the offender's culpability and the gravity of his crime – then there is no scientific means, and probably no human means, of telling whether the sentence in question is appropriate, excessive or lenient.

At the other extreme, some objectives lend themselves to easy measurement. If the aim is to compel the offender to compensate his victim for loss or damage to property, it is not too hard to tell whether this is in fact achieved. Similarly, if the aim is to prevent certain offenders from repeating their offences, the success of preventive sentences of imprisonment can be measured by the escape rate. Some reservations must be made here. The offender may go on offending inside prison: one of the ridiculous features of imprisonment for private homosexual conduct between consenting adults was that it made it easier for some to indulge in this. Again, some sentences which are said by the sentencer to be for the protection of society are so short that they represent only a fraction of the offender's active life, and merely succeed in postponing his next offence for a short period. Some preventive sentences, however, present a more difficult problem of measurement. The obvious example is disqualification from holding or obtaining a driving licence. Not only are most disqualifications for short periods during which nothing is done to improve the offender's driving, but an unknown and probably substantial number of disqualified drivers continue to drive, in many cases without detection, although the new computerized index of licences should help the police to reduce the prevalence of this.

Deterrent Efficacy

The two main problems in this area, however, are concerned with the efficacy of general deterrents and of corrective measures.[1] Let us first consider general deterrents, that is, measures which are either *intended* (as fines are) to discourage potential offenders from offending, or at least *believed* to do so, whatever the main intention of the measure is or was (capital punishment being an example).

The very nature of the process of deterrence makes its operation hard to study objectively. While a deterrent is in operation it is difficult, if not altogether impracticable, to devise a satisfactory way of finding out the number of occasions on which it has been the decisive consideration in the mind of a person who rejected an opportunity for law breaking.

Moreover, we are seldom, if ever, in a position to measure what can be called the 'absolute efficacy' of a deterrent by comparing a situation in which there is *no* deterrent with a situation in which there is *only that* deterrent. This is sometimes forgotten in discussions of the effect of abolishing or reimposing a type of penalty, such as capital or corporal punishment; and the fact that 'abolition' really means 'replacement with long sentences of imprisonment' is overlooked. For this reason, the most that we can usually hope to measure is 'comparative efficacy', that is, the extent to which a given deterrent is more effective than the alternatives to it.

1. These terms are preferable to the looser ones 'preventive' and 'reformative' measures. The former leads to confusion with such measures as preventive custody or even eugenics. The latter can be understood as excluding the deterrence of the individual who experiences the sentence, and thus begs the question whether its efficacy is due to individual deterrence or to a genuine improvement in his character – a point about which it is seldom possible to be sure. Confusion and question begging can be reduced to the minimum by using 'general deterrence' to exclude 'individual deterrence', and 'correction' to include both 'reformation' and 'individual deterrence'.

Even when we are fortunate enough to find a situation in which some type of conduct has recently been made criminal, and punishable with a more or less specific penalty, such as a fine, we are seldom in a position to answer the question 'How frequent was it before it became punishable?' since it is not until conduct becomes a crime that police begin to keep statistical records of it.

Essentials for Assessment

Only in rather special conditions is it possible to make even cautious inferences from official statistics. The necessary conditions are that:

1. Statistics of the frequency with which a given type of offence is reported must be kept in a uniform way over a period.

2. During this period the penalties for the offence must be changed, whether by statute or by an alteration in sentencing policy. The sharper the change the better from the scientist's point of view.

3. This change must be publicized.

4. It must not coincide with any other development that is likely to affect the frequency of the offence in question (such as an increase or decrease in opportunities, or in police activity).

5. The probability of incurring the usual penalty for the commission of the offence must be fairly high.

The relevance of most of these conditions seems obvious, but they are easily overlooked. For example, a 1968 report by the Assembly Office of Research to the Californian legislature cites a study of the bad cheque problem in Nebraska and other States (Beutel, 1957) in support of the statement that regional variations in the severity of penalties have no effect on crime rates. The study had certainly demonstrated that in Colorado and other States where penalties for bad cheques were more lenient, prosecutions for this type of offence were relatively *less* common. It had also disclosed, however, how few bad cheques were ever brought to the notice of the law: the percentage in the Nebraska sample was about 2 per cent! If the chance of actually incurring the penalty was as low as this,[2] it is hardly surprising that the

2. In fact it was even less, because a substantial percentage of cases reported to law-enforcement officers were settled unofficially by payment of the debt.

difference between a short and a medium term of imprisonment seemed to have no effect in reducing the frequency of the offence.

The importance of ensuring that publicity is given to any changes in the penalty is illustrated by a Finnish experiment (Tornudd, 1968). This is one of the very few instances in which social scientists have been able to persuade agencies of law enforcement to alter their policy as a deliberate test of a penological hypothesis. This one was concerned with the offence of public drunkenness. Drunks are notoriously apt to reappear in court again and again for this offence, a fact which casts doubt on the effectiveness of fining and imprisonment as deterrents in their case. In Finland, where police not only make the arrests but also decide in the first place whether the drunk should be fined[3] (subject to confirmation by the court), the police forces in three medium-sized towns were persuaded to reduce the percentages which were fined in the three years 1962–4. In one of the towns the percentage of arrests for drunkenness which led to fines was reduced from more than 50 to less than 20 per cent, and the reductions in the other two, though less spectacular, were very marked. Three similar towns were used as controls, and in them the fining percentages remained fairly stable, between 50 and 60 per cent.

In the first year of the experiment the rate of arrests for drunkenness remained much the same as they had been in the experimental towns. In the second year there was a sharp rise in one of the towns, almost certainly the result of a new highway project which brought many migrant workers – often heavy drinkers – to the area; the rates in the other two towns did not increase, and if anything were a little below average. Two of the control towns showed slight increases, one showed a marked decrease!

In short, there were no changes in the rates – in an upward or downward direction – which could be attributed to the experimental reduction in the percentage of arrests leading to fines. Unfortunately, it had been deliberately decided[4] not to publicize the reduction, and investigators who mixed with the chronic drunks in the experimental towns found that in fact they had not guessed that there had been a change

3. As in England, failure to pay the fine – which is frequent – almost always leads to imprisonment for a short period.

4. Perhaps because the police were afraid of the public's reaction; but the reason for the decision is not explained.

of policy; those who were released by the police without a fine simply explained their good luck by saying 'I suppose I wasn't so drunk after all.' All that the experiment demonstrated, therefore, was that even a marked change in sentencing policy, lasting for at least three years, did not seem to have been noticed by the offenders directly affected.

A Good Experiment

The nearest approach to a sound and successful experiment in testing a deterrent is probably that achieved by R. Schwartz and Sonya D. Orleans, with the help of the United States Internal Revenue Service. Nearly 400 taxpayers were divided into four matched groups. Members of the 'sanction' group were interviewed and asked questions designed to remind them indirectly of the penalties which they might suffer if they tried to evade taxes. Members of the 'conscience' group were interviewed with questions designed to arouse their civic sense and feelings of duty. The third, or 'placebo' group were asked only neutral questions, which avoided both sorts of stimulus. The fourth group were not interviewed at all, in order to test the possibility that even a 'placebo' interview produced some effect (which on the whole it did not seem to do). The interviews took place in the month before the taxpayers were due to file their returns for 1962. Without disclosing information about individuals, the Internal Revenue Service compared the returns of the four groups for the year before the experiment and the year 1962. The reported gross incomes of both the 'sanction' and the 'conscience' groups showed an increase, compared with small *decreases* in the 'placebo' and 'uninterviewed' groups. In other words, the attempts to stimulate both fear of penalties and civic conscience seemed to have had effect.[5]

Negative Evidence

For an example of negative evidence, let us turn to the well-known controversy over the efficacy of capital punishment as a deterrent for potential murderers, which has led to several statistical studies of

5. See Schwartz and Orleans (1967). They drew a slightly bolder conclusion: that appeals to conscience were *more* effective than threat of sanctions; but this inference assumes that the appeal and the threat were of equal potency, whereas it is conceivable that unintentionally they had made their 'conscience' interview a more powerful stimulus.

murder rates. Those worth considering have either compared contemporary rates in areas which do and areas which do not make use of the death penalty, but which have roughly similar definitions of murder; or compared rates for the same country during periods when the death penalty was and was not used. The best example of the first sort of study is Sellin's comparison of abolitionist and retentionist States of the USA, to be found in the appendixes to the *Report of the Royal Commission on Capital Punishment, 1949–53*. For a study of the latter sort, see Walker (1965, p. 240) and in particular the graph (reproduced here as Figure 6) of New Zealand's murder rate from 1924–62, a period during which capital punishment was at first in force, then in abeyance, then abolished, then restored, then in abeyance and then abolished again. Although New Zealand was not deliberately experimenting, the result of its changes of policy is as close as we are likely to come to an experimental use of the death penalty. The changes were well publicized throughout this small country (as were the cases in which the death penalty was actually carried out); and murder is a crime which is solved more often than any other.

Neither New Zealand nor American data suggest the hypothesis that, as a deterrent, capital punishment is more effective than the long periods of imprisonment which take its place in abolitionist jurisdictions. It is equally important, however, to appreciate what this does not prove. In the first place, these studies relate to areas with relatively low murder rates. It is possible that other factors have reduced the rates in both abolitionist and retentionist jurisdictions or periods to a point at which further reduction would be very difficult to achieve. An analogy is the prevalence of tuberculosis, which is easy to reduce when it is high, but not at all easy to reduce beyond a certain low level. Although it sounds a paradoxical hypothesis, it is by no means unlikely that capital punishment is a more effective deterrent in countries with high murder rates.

Another assertion which is not supported by the data, even for countries with low murder rates, is that nobody is deterred from murder by the thought of the death penalty who would not be equally deterred by the thought of long imprisonment. All that the data suggest is that in countries with low murder rates such people are not numerous enough for their murders to be detectable among fluctuations which are due to other factors.

Negative Evidence   95

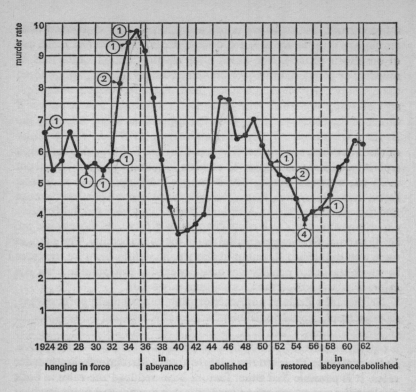

- moving 5-year averages [for meaning of 'moving average' see Appendix A, page 139] per million inhabitants of murders known to the police
- number of executions carried out in the year

Figure 6 Murder rates and the death penalty in New Zealand (from Walker, 1969, p. 60)

The Burden of Proof

Most important of all, such studies provide no justification whatsoever for the sweeping assumption that other forms of general deterrent are ineffective. This is due to a loose sequence of reasoning, which seems to go like this:

1. We must not accept any statement unless and until it is supported by sound statistical evidence.

96 Measuring Deterrent Efficacy

2. The only statistical evidence we have about general deterrents is the evidence about capital punishment, which suggests that its effectiveness in civilized countries at least is negligible.

3. We must not, therefore, act on the assumption that such measures as fines or imprisonment serve as general deterrents.

The main flaw in the argument is the way in which it begins by talking of 'accepting' statements and ends by talking of 'acting on' them. If the first assertion means that it is desirable to question any important assumption until it is supported by statistically sound evidence, it is an excellent principle for the social scientist. But if it means that we should not base social policy on that assumption until the scientists have pronounced it confirmed, this is contrary to common sense. It would be rational only if we were faced with a choice between courses of action, knowing only that one course was beneficial and the other detrimental, but not knowing which was which. In matters of social policy this is hardly ever the situation. Almost always we have some grounds for predicting the outcomes of our choices. At worst these grounds consist of our own experience and self-knowledge, as when we say 'Well, I know that I am deterred from illegal parking by the thought of a stiff fine.' More often we have the benefit of the experience of others, although not in a statistically satisfactory form. In this situation it is certainly desirable that some social scientist should try to find a way of appraising this experience statistically, or of testing our belief in an experimental situation. What is not reasonable is to allege that until he does so we have *no* grounds for acting on our own prediction of the outcomes of the choices. To use a lawyer's phrase, if a social scientist sets out to undermine a belief which is at present based on crude experience, then the burden of proof lies on him.

What the social scientists have done is to question effectively the time-honoured belief that capital punishment keeps down the murder rate. So far as societies with low murder rates are concerned they have succeeded in shifting the onus of proof on to those who, for some reason, wish to cling to the belief. But murder is one of the rarest of crimes. To what extent can conclusions about murder be applied to other sorts of offence? It is not unreasonable to apply them to offences of serious personal violence, since many of these occur in the same situations as murders, spring from the same motives and, indeed, often differ from murders only accidentally – for example, because the knife or the bullet missed an artery, or because the victim reached hospital in time for a blood transfusion or brain surgery.

What is unreasonable is to apply the same conclusions to other types of offences such as bad driving or theft, which have nothing in common with murder beyond the fact that they are committed by human beings and are triable by criminal courts. One might as well argue that because few chess-players bet on their games, few card-players probably do so. The Illinois experiment supported the common-sense assumption that taxpayers respond to the threat of sanctions. The impossibility, however, of applying the same technique to other everyday offences, such as theft, is obvious, and it must be plain from the preceding discussion how unlikely we are to find sound evidence of the efficacy of deterrents in routine statistics. Failing this, we are entitled to consider what can be learned by other methods.

A Survey of Young Men

One is the interviewing of potential offenders. An interesting example of this is the subject of a report by the Government Social Survey (Willcock and Stokes, 1968). Since young males in the second half of their teens and early twenties are the age group with the highest rates of serious crime, the Home Office asked the Government Social Survey to interview a sample of youths whose ages ranged from fifteen to twenty-two. This was done in 1963, and the sample obtained was 808. Sixteen per cent had been in court, accused of an offence of some kind, serious or trivial; three out of four had met someone to whom this had happened. Whether or not they had been brought to court for it, 17 per cent admitted at least one theft,[6] 20 per cent admitted having taken part at least once in vandalism or gang fighting, and 84 per cent admitted traffic offences. Although these percentages are no doubt smaller than they would have been if every member of the sample had been completely frank, it is clear that these males at a delinquency-prone age were a mixture of the deterred and undeterred.

Factual information apart, what someone says in response to a questionnaire or interviewer may not be a reliable indication of the

6. Including taking and driving away a motor vehicle.

98 Measuring Deterrent Efficacy

way in which he will think and act when faced with a real situation of the kind which he is talking about. Consequently what these 808 young males said about the considerations which would or would not deter them from offences cannot be accepted without reservations. Nevertheless, this is a case where some information – so long as it is obtained with care, as this was – is better than no information.

Although the Willcock and Stokes's sample was questioned about a fairly wide range of offences[7] let us for the moment at least confine ourselves to one type of crime, of a kind which is usually attributable to a rational motive, and which can hardly be committed without a deliberate decision to attempt it, so that anyone contemplating an attempt at it might be expected to take any deterrents into consideration. House-breaking is an obvious choice. It is one of the commonest forms of acquisitive crime, and appears to be especially attractive to young men of the age group represented in this sample. It has the additional advantage of being separately dealt with in the *Criminal Statistics*, so that objective, if rough, estimates can be made of the probability of detection and its consequences.

Consider the young man of twenty-one to whom it has occurred to break into a house. One likely possibility is that he would decide against doing so for reasons which are not connected with deterrents. He might be restrained by what is sometimes called 'conscience', sometimes 'super-ego', sometimes 'self-image' and sometimes by the deliberately vague term 'internal restraints'. In the Willcock and Stokes's sample 44 per cent gave a reason of this kind which, they said, would hold them back or at least worry them. Another 3 per cent seemed simply to lack confidence in their ability to commit a competent break-in. And 40 per cent seemed to be more concerned about the consequences of being identified as criminals, although – as we shall see – it was not necessarily the official consequences which they had in mind.

How high did they rate the chances of detection? Objectively the *Criminal Statistics* show that only about one-third of house-breakings are 'cleared up', a phrase which almost always means 'traced to a suspect', although this does not always imply prosecution (see Chapter

7. 'Starting a punch-up', 'breaking into a private house', 'stealing from a large store', 'stealing from a small shop', 'breaking into a lock-up shop', 'taking and driving away a car', 'stealing from a coat' and 'picking up a wallet'.

3.) In other words, the general risk of detection in a single shop breaking is something less than one in three: and for certain sub-groups – such as the young man of normal intelligence – it must be lower still. Among the Willcock and Stokes's sample, however, estimates of the risk varied widely. Most of them thought that their chances of 'getting away' with burglary were less than fifty-fifty; some were very pessimistic indeed. Less than one-fifth gave anything like a realistic estimate. In other words, most of the sample greatly over-estimated their chances of being caught.

There was some evidence, however, that the more experience a youth had of committing offences the more optimistic he tended to be about the chances of getting away with them. And, of course, in the case of the sort of offence which we are considering optimism meant realism. The point is important, because one of the commonest platitudes on the subject of law enforcement is that the best hope for improving it lies in increasing the probability of detection. So far as house-breakings (and most other acquisitive crimes) are concerned this is a visionary's hope. The clear-up rate is so low that it is over-estimated by all but a small minority. To alter the estimates of the realistic minority would require an enormous increase in police efficiency; and to raise still further the over-estimates of the majority seems almost out of the question.

On the other hand, we do know that a sudden and well-publicized lowering of police efficiency can lead to a sharp increase in some types of offence. For seven months in 1944 the Danish police force was under arrest by the German occupation troops, with the result that robberies and larcenies multiplied in a spectacular way (while crimes such as fraud and embezzlement did not!) (Andenaes, 1966; Trolle, 1945). In England the strike of the Liverpool police in 1919 was accompanied by widespread looting; and there are similar accounts of the effects of police strikes elsewhere (for example in Melbourne).

Detection does not, of course, mean automatic conviction. It is true that most acquisitive offenders plead guilty, especially if by doing so they can make it likely that they will be sentenced by a magistrate's court, with its limited sentencing powers. If, however, they plead not guilty before a jury, their chances of an acquittal are by no means negligible; as was seen in Chapter 6, a survey of jury acquittals in 1969 showed a probability of about 40 per cent where the charges involved burglary or robbery. The Willcock and Stokes's sample was not asked for its estimates of the probability that detection would lead to conviction, but it seems likely that the more experienced it was the higher it would rate its chances of an acquittal.

Prosecution and its Consequences

What the sample was asked about was the assumed consequences of appearing in court. It was shown, in random order, eight cards each describing a possible consequence, and asked, 'Which of these things would worry you most about being found out by the police?', after which each youth sorted the cards into his order of importance. Table 16 shows the result.

Table 16

	Mean rank	% placing item first
1. What my family would think about it	2·38	49
2. The chances of losing my job	2·96	22
3. Publicity or shame of having to appear in court	3·88	12
4. The punishment I might get	4·40	10
5. What my girl friend would think	4·72	6
6. Whether I should get fair treatment in court	6·07	2
7. What my mates would think	6·08	1
8. What might happen to me between being found out and appearing in court	6·20	2

There are several striking features in this table. 'What my family would think' is far and away the most important consideration. Next is the possibility of losing one's job. Considerably less important was public exposure in court, and slightly less important than that was the official penalty. The other items were relatively negligible.

We cannot, of course, conclude that the operative deterrent for about half of the sample was the thought of their families' reaction. For we must remember that almost as many (43 per cent) had said that they would have been held back from law-breaking, or at least worried, by 'conscience' or some other form of internal restraint. And since the sort of family which reacts strongly against law breaking is also the sort of family which is likely to have sons with strong internal restraints, many of the youths who put their families' reactions at the top of their lists of deterrents must have been youths who would in fact have been held back by internal restraints. Nevertheless, Willcock and Stokes found that even youths who had committed a wide variety of offences seemed to rank these disincentives in much the same order as did their more innocent colleagues, giving top place on the whole to the same unofficial consequences of detection.

We must, however, pay some attention to the deterrents which are within the power of the courts to impose. Not surprisingly, the great majority (81 per cent) of the sample ranked prison as the penalty which they most feared. Borstals were ranked first by a much smaller percentage (13 per cent), and next came approved schools and detention centres. What was surprising was that a fine seemed to be regarded as a less formidable deterrent than probation, although this is certainly not the assumption upon which courts or probation officers make their decisions. Yet when one looks at the choice from the point of view of a young man, it is not difficult to understand how the prospect of two or three years' supervision by someone whom he regards as representing authority (and rightly) is more unpleasant than the loss of one or two weeks' wages (few of the youths expected the fine to be more than £25, and some expected much less).

That is by the way, however: we must get back to the custodial penalties which were at the top of the list. We cannot infer from this that they operate as the most powerful deterrents unless we know that potential offenders consider them probable results of being convicted. The sample was asked what was the 'worst' penalty which it expected someone to get for offences such as shop breaking or joy riding in an unknown person's car: it was told to distinguish between someone with no criminal record and someone with a bad record. Since a custodial sentence of one sort or another is not only a possible penalty in both cases, but is actually imposed on a minority of first offenders of this age group (and, of course, more often still on offenders with previous records), it was interesting to see that over 60 per cent of the sample gave a fine or a probation order as their answer. It hardly matters whether they really meant that a custodial penalty was out of the question; for them it was not a serious possibility.

Since a fine or a probation order are in fact the most likely outcomes for 'first offenders', it is difficult to argue that these respondents were being over-optimistic, still less that by ensuring that they were better informed we should ensure that they were better behaved. In other words, only a sharp and well-publicized increase in the frequency of custodial sentences for a 'first offender' could conceivably render them effective as general deterrents for potential but inexperienced offenders. This would be so directly contrary to present ideas on the sentencing of first offenders, which are not without some rational foundation (as we shall see), that the case for it would have to be overwhelming before it could be seriously advocated.

Where offenders with previous convictions are concerned, the probability of a custodial sentence is already considerably higher, as most of the sample recognized, although there were substantial minorities (14 per cent in the case of house-breaking) who still thought that probation or a fine were the worst that could be expected in such cases. We do not know how high it really is after the second, third or nth conviction; still less how high the experienced shop breaker thinks it is. The more knowledgeable he is, however, the more optimistic he is likely to be about his chances of escaping conviction. As we have seen, the general probability of escaping detection for this type of offence is over two in three, and when this is multiplied by the not altogether negligible chance of an acquittal if the house-breaker appears before a jury, he does not have to be over-optimistic to regard the prospect of a custodial sentence as unlikely. (As we saw in Chapter 3, it is true that a probability of two in three for a single house-breaking falls to four in nine for a couple of house-breakings, to eight in twenty-seven for three, and so on, geometrically; but house-breakers are not conversant with the mathematics of probability.) This being so, it would require a very considerable increase in the percentage of shop-breakers with previous convictions who receive custodial sentences to make any impression on them.

Chapter 13
Measuring
Corrective Efficacy

When trying to assess the efficacy of a corrective measure, the main difficulty is to agree upon the sort of things that are to be accepted as signs of correction. If all that is claimed for a penal measure is that it produces deterred or reformed offenders, or a mixture of these, then by definition this will have been achieved if offenders who would have continued to break the law refrain in some or all cases from doing so as a result of the measure, or at least do so less frequently. But if it is claimed that a certain penal measure produces *morally improved* offenders, or that at least some of its products are morally improved, the criteria by which such a claim can be verified are more difficult to agree upon. Breaches of the law can be counted, at least in theory, but on what sort of scales is virtue weighed? What notation does the Recording Angel use? If, as most people would agree, no objective standard can be offered, then it must be left to the fallible judgments of mortals. But which of us is to say whether an offender is morally improved? Not the offender himself; even if he could be sure, which is doubtful, he is at least as much of a hypocrite as the rest of us, and if he thinks it will make us happier or cut short his punishment he will assure us that he is a better man. Not the probation officer, psychiatrist nor prison officer; although they at least know what sort of moral improvement they were trying to achieve, it is a very exceptional man who can be an impartial judge of his own success or failure. Moreover, it is only the exceptional psychiatrist or probation officer who keeps in touch for long with patients or probationers for whom he is no longer responsible. Sometimes it is possible to get a reasonably unbiased report from an offender's wife, or parent or near relative; but even then it is hard to be sure that their standards are those of the psychiatrist or probation officer.

This ideological issue is important because there is a school of thought which rejects mere breaches of the law as adequate criteria of reformation. Perhaps the best exposition of this point of view is to be found in the Morison report on the probation service (Departmental Committee on the Probation Service, 1962):

But the avoidance of offences is a poor, and even *misleading*[1] measure of the rehabilitation of the offender and of the degree to which he had learnt to overcome anti-social traits and attitudes, to live happily within the limitations imposed by society, and to meet, or reconcile himself to, material and environmental difficulties that accompanied and, perhaps, occasioned his delinquent behaviour. Conversely, the commission of another offence may mark no more than a temporary relapse in the rehabilitative process. Further, on a wholly material level, it is difficult to regard the offence as showing a total failure with the probationer if, in the period of supervision, he has met difficulties to which he would otherwise have given way or accepted responsibilities which he would otherwise have avoided. No penal treatment can do more than the delinquent's limitations permit and with many offenders periodic breakdowns in behaviour must be expected.

In order to dismiss the evidence of subsequent law-breaking in this way, it is necessary to believe that it is not merely an *inadequate* criterion but also a *misleading* one; and while the Morison Committee actually use the word 'misleading' it is by no means certain that they appreciated the distinction.

In order to be able to say that the statistics of subsequent law breaking are *misleading* one must be prepared to demonstrate, with evidence, that if one divided up the offenders into those who have subsequently broken the law and those who have not, those who had *broken* the law would actually include *more* of the morally improved. In more scientific terms, one would have to show that law-breaking was positively associated with moral improvement in the wider sense. In everyday terms, it is up to the person who rejects statistics of reconvictions to prove that the reconvicted man is likely to be morally better than the man who has 'kept out of trouble'. Until convincing evidence of this is produced, the reasonable assumption is that by using statistics of law-breaking we shall have an imperfect but by no means useless way of identifying most of the men who have been reformed in the most ambitious sense. The rest of this chapter proceeds on the

1. Author's italics.

common-sense assumption that such statistics are the only scientific test which we can at present apply to corrective measures.

Incompleteness of Reconvictions

I do not mean to gloss over several defects which have to be kept in mind when reconvictions are used as an index. The most serious defect is, of course, their incompleteness, that is, the percentage of offenders who, though not reconvicted, have committed further offences. Since less than half the thefts known to the police are traced to the thief, the 'incompleteness' of the reconvictions of thieves must be considerable. This factor of incompleteness is of course much smaller in the case of certain types of offences, such as cases of serious violence, of which over 85 per cent are cleared up.

Elusiveness of Reconvictions

A second though much less important defect of reconvictions is the difficulty of being certain that even if an offender is reconvicted his reconviction is traced. Let us call the percentage of convictions which are not traced the 'elusiveness rate'. This is smallest in the case of convictions of adults for indictable offences, since there is a fairly efficient system for collecting a national record of these. Every conviction of a person over seventeen for an indictable offence is reported (in theory, at least) with the offender's name and other identifying information, to the Criminal Records Office at New Scotland Yard, where a search is made for any previous convictions of the same person for indictable offences. If any are found, the latest is associated with them. Thus the CRO index should show any subsequent convictions for serious offences of someone who has already been subjected to any penal measure (including a discharge) for a serious offence. Moreover, the system even records some offences of which a former offender is strongly suspected but has not been convicted. It is possible that the use of aliases may introduce a small element of elusiveness, but the fingerprint system must keep this to a very low level. What the system does not attempt to collate is two categories of offence:

1. Most non-indictable offences. If a magistrates' court convicts a person over seventeen of an offence for which he could have been

tried at a higher court, the conviction is reported to the CRO. If it is not one for which he could have been so tried, then with a few exceptions it is not reported. The exceptions are important, for they include the non-indictable forms of the indictable offences, and for this reason are sometimes called 'quasi-indictable'. Thus, non-indictable sexual offences, such as indecent exposure, are also reported. On the other hand, no non-indictable motoring offences or offences of drunkenness or any of the hundred and one other transgressions with which magistrates must deal summarily are reported.

2. Most offences by juveniles. Offences committed by juveniles within the London Metropolitan Police District are reported to the CRO; but some other areas report only the most serious offences by persons under seventeen, such as murder, attempted murder, or rape. As a result, childhood exploits of a provincial thief are not usually recorded there, although the information can usually be obtained from the probation department and the children's department of the areas in which he is known to have lived.

Finally, the elusiveness of pre-1945 convictions is undoubtedly greater for all kinds of offence and offender. Before and during the war, reporting to CRO by local police forces was less complete. As children's departments of local authorities did not officially exist before 1948, few of them have records of children which extend before that date. Probation departments' pre-war records also tend to be scanty. In consequence a middle-aged recidivist's early convictions are very elusive, unless he himself is both communicative and gifted with total recall.

The Success Rate

In spite of these defects, and another which I shall discuss next, claims for the corrective efficacy of penal measures are frequently based on what is called the 'success rate'. When looked at closely, this is found to consist of some sample of offenders who have been subjected to, say, imprisonment, *minus* those who are known to have been reconvicted. It will be obvious from what has been said that the remainder, though classified as 'successes', will contain an unknown number who have in fact committed further offences but because of the incompleteness or the elusiveness of reconvictions have not been classified as reconvicted. It is more honest and precise to base such claims on 'the known reconviction percentage'.

Follow-Up Periods

Even the phrase 'known reconviction percentage', however, is not as precise as it could be. Few criminal careers are followed to the grave, so that in fact most figures for reconvictions simply represent those which occurred within some period. The most misleading are those which deal with offenders released at widely different dates but represent reconvictions occurring up to a single date. Since the offenders have been 'at risk' of reconviction for differing periods, such a reconviction percentage must be interpreted with caution, unless the periods are very long indeed.[2] Otherwise, the 'follow-up' period should be roughly equal for each offender. The question how long it should be is also important. No investigation has yet followed enough criminal careers to the bitter end to be able to say that if an offender is going to be reconvicted this will happen within a definite number of years. In W. H. Hammond's eleven-year follow-up of Scottish first offenders it was observed that of those who were reconvicted during that period, 65 per cent were reconvicted by the end of the third year after the year of release from prison, probation, etc.[3] For recidivists the same period would include an even higher percentage of those who would be reconvicted at some date. In this way it is possible to state two rules:

1. The higher the percentage of first offenders in the sample, the longer the follow-up ought to be; conversely, the higher the percentage or degree of recidivism, the shorter it can be.

2. But if for some reason a short period of follow-up has to be accepted, reconviction percentages during the first year 'at risk' will show whether a longer follow-up is likely to yield substantial differences, provided of course that the sample is large enough to render the differences significant.[4]

2. As they were in W. H. Hammond's Glasgow investigation: see below.
3. Personal communication from W. H. Hammond.
4. This probability should certainly not exceed 1 per cent.

There is an increasing tendency in British research to insist on a follow-up period of at least two years, and it seems likely that for most purposes three years may become standard. From the point of view of interpretation of results it is obviously necessary to make sure that one is not comparing reconviction percentages based on differing follow-up periods. For precision, therefore, it is desirable to refer to 'known (three)-year reconviction percentages', and for complete precision, to 'known (three)-year reconviction percentages for indictable and quasi-indictable offences (after age seventeen)'. In other words, reports of follow-up of criminal careers must make it clear exactly what they are reporting.

It is also important to know how thorough the follow-up has been. It will be clear from what has been said about the elusiveness of reconvictions that a follow-up of offenders under the age of seventeen which relies only on the Criminal Records Office would be most unsatisfactory, just as a follow-up of an adult which did not use CRO would also be incomplete.

The Spontaneous Recovery Rate

Let us suppose that we have, as a result of a thorough follow-up, a known three-year reconviction percentage for indictable and quasi-indictable offences in the case of a properly selected sample of offenders. There is one more difficulty to be circumvented. Even if we are reasonably confident that those in the sample who are not reported as reconvicted have in fact 'gone straight', we are not entitled to assume that this is the result of any penal treatment to which they have been subjected unless we can also claim to know how many of them would have gone straight even if not subjected to any penal treatment. Not only do many first offenders who are found guilty but are discharged, absolutely or conditionally, seem to avoid subsequent reconviction, but it is also extremely probable that, even if not detected, a substantial percentage of people commit one or two offences and then spontaneously stop. In other words, we have here very much the same factor to reckon with as psychiatrists have – what is called the 'spontaneous recovery rate' – with the unfortunate difference that whereas psychologists such as Eysenck claim to be able to make at least a rough estimate of the size of this factor in the case of certain groups of mental illnesses, it would be a bold penologist who would make this claim in the case of offenders. As we shall see, however, there is a certain amount of indirect evidence for the existence of a 'spontaneous reform rate' among offenders.

Absolute and Comparative Efficacy

This means that when discussing corrective efficacy we must distinguish between 'absolute' and 'comparative' efficacy. The absolute corrective efficacy of a given measure is the margin by which the percentage of offenders who are corrected by it exceeds the percentage who would not have repeated their offences even if they had remained undetected. Its comparative efficacy is the margin by which the corrected percentage exceeds that of some other specified measure, for example discharge.

Nobody has yet contrived to assess the absolute efficacy of a penal measure, and the difficulties of doing so are obvious. As for comparative efficacy, even attempts to assess this must avoid at least one fallacy: the comparison of independent studies. Several post-war studies have traced reconvictions, usually for indictable and quasi-indictable offences, following various types of penal measures.[5] But since they were independent studies, with follow-up periods of varying lengths, and using samples of offenders whose ages, types of offence, previous convictions and other penal characteristics were not matched, they provide no basis for estimates of the comparative efficacy of the measures studied. Rather, what emerges from a general survey of this literature is the importance of a few variables:

1. In practically all studies, the fewer the previous convictions the lower the subsequent conviction rate.

2. The older the offender during the follow-up period the lower the reconviction rate.

3. The more time he has spent in custodial institutions the more likely he is to be reconvicted.

4. Women and girls have lower reconviction rates than men or boys of comparable age and penal history.

5. The main independent reconviction studies are listed in *The Sentence of the Court* (Home Office, 1969). The Prison Department's annual *Statistical Tables* show reconvictions, within stated periods at risk, of certain categories of prisoners.

5. Offenders whose crimes are of different types probably have different reconviction rates even after the same kind of penal measure is applied. For example, adult males who have committed heterosexual offences against girls under sixteen are apparently less likely to be reconvicted of sexual offences after imprisonment or probation than adult males who have been convicted of homosexual offences against boys or youths under twenty-one, even when those with and those without previous convictions for sexual offences are separately compared. Drunkenness probably has a particularly high reconviction rate.

From our point of view the most important inference to be drawn from these observations is that any attempt to estimate the comparative efficacy of one sort of penal measure by comparing reconvictions after it with reconvictions after another sort must be regarded as unreliable unless some way can be found of eliminating, or at least reducing to negligible proportions, the effects of at least the following variables – the offender's sex, age, previous criminal career, and type of offence. Indeed, it would be possible to be even more rigorous and add other variables, such as the time which the offender has spent in custodial institutions of any sort and, if the follow-up periods do not begin and end with the same calendar year, fluctuations in the annual conviction rate for the age groups under study. Very few published studies meet those requirements, but there are two which both illustrate the possibilities of two different statistical methods and at the same time have yielded interesting results.

Probation versus the Rest

A striking use of the matching technique for this purpose was L. T. Wilkins's (1958) comparison of the results of probation with the results of other penal measures. A court of Quarter Sessions (called Court 'P') was selected because it used probation in a very high percentage of its cases (three times the national average). Ninety-seven males dealt with by that court in 1952 by means of probation, prison, Borstal or fine were matched one for one with ninety-seven other male offenders, selected from those dealt with by 194 other courts in such a way that each one corresponded as closely as possible to his 'mate' in (a) type of offence, (b) age of offender, (c) number of additional convictions at the same appearance, (d) number of additional offences 'taken into consideration', and (e) number of previous convictions for indictable offences[6]

Reconvictions for indictable and quasi-indictable offences were traced for the three years following sentence.[7]

The results can be summarized thus:

1. Court P put fifty out of its ninety-seven cases on probation. But out of the fifty matched controls in the other courts, only nineteen were put on probation; instead, twenty-four were sent to prison or Borstal, six were fined and one discharged. Nevertheless, the percentages reconvicted were very similar for both courts – 40 per cent for Court P, 44 per cent for the other courts.

2. Court P sent forty of its ninety-seven cases to prison or Borstal; out of the forty matched controls, most (i.e. thirty-three) were dealt with similarly, though four were put on probation, two discharged and one fined. Nevertheless, exactly 50 per cent of both groups of forty were reconvicted.

3. The number fined by Court P was very small – seven; none were reconvicted. Of the controls, three went to prison or Borstal, two were discharged, one was fined, one put on probation; two were reconvicted but it is not stated which.

What Wilkins thus did was to cast doubt on the assertion that if probation were applied wholesale to males over seventeen in place of fines, prison and Borstal, the reconviction rates would be markedly less. What he did not do, nor claim to have done, was to cast any doubt on the absolute efficacy of any of these measures. His results are equally consistent with the hypothesis that the absolute efficacy of probation is considerable and with the hypothesis that it is very low, or nil. But whatever the truth may be, the absolute efficacy of prison and Borstal seems to be roughly the same.

6. On the whole, however, Court P's offenders had worse records, since their previous convictions totalled seventy-two, with a maximum of twenty-five for one offender, while the controls had only forty-three between them, and a maximum of five.

7. A slight defect was that those sentenced to prison and Borstal were 'at risk' for a shorter time, since they were in custody for some of the three years. But since most of the prison sentences were for only a few months, the bias in favour of those so dealt with was slight. Only the Borstal boys were likely to have been 'inside' for more than a few months.

The Use of 'Expectation'

The use of matched samples has disadvantages. In particular, one-for-one matching entails the discarding of individuals who cannot be matched with a member of another sample, either because of unusual characteristics or because of unequal numbers; and if more than two groups have to be matched the percentage of discards rises. This both wastes information and disregards the extreme case. A method which avoids these disadvantages is the calculation of 'expected' reconvictions for a given penal measure, and the comparison of these with the number of actual reconvictions of the offenders subjected to that measure.

An imaginary example illustrates the method in its simplest form. Suppose that of 200 males half are fined, half imprisoned, with the following results in terms of known reconvictions over the next three years at risk:

$$\text{fined 100: reconvicted: 40}$$
imprisoned 100: reconvicted: 70

A second analysis shows that, irrespective of the penal measure used, younger men were more often reconvicted:

under 30   120: reconvicted: $80 (= \frac{2}{3})$
  over 30   80: reconvicted: $30 (= \frac{3}{8})$

A third analysis shows that these two age groups were unevenly distributed between the fined men and the imprisoned men:

$$\text{fined 100: under 30: 80}$$
$$\text{over 30: 20}$$
imprisoned 100: under 30: 40
over 30: 60

Thus, if age were the only variable which had an effect upon reconvictions, the following reconvictions would be expected:

fined: $\frac{2}{3}$ of the 80 men under 30 = 53 $\left.\right\}$ = 61
$\quad\quad\frac{3}{8}$ of the 20 men over   30 =   8

imprisoned: $\frac{2}{3}$ of the 40 men under 30 = 26 $\left.\right\}$ = 49
$\quad\quad\quad\quad\frac{3}{8}$ of the 60 men over   30 = 23

On this basis, the expected reconvictions for the fined men would be sixty-one, compared with an actual number of forty: and for imprisonment the expectation would be forty-nine, compared with an actual seventy. It is convenient to express the actual reconvictions as percentages of the expected number, thus:

fined: 66 per cent of expectation (i.e. $\frac{40}{61}$)

imprisoned: 143 per cent of expectation (i.e. $\frac{70}{49}$)

The assumption underlying this technique is that the difference between these percentages is a measure of the comparative efficacy of the two different penal measures, so far as offenders of this sort (in this case, males) are concerned. The assumption is obviously unrealistic when only one variable – in this case, age – is used to calculate expected reconvictions, and when the comparison is limited to two penal measures. But the same method can in theory be extended to take into account any number of variables, and any number of penal measures; the only limiting condition is that the numbers of individuals in each of the necessary subdivisions should be substantial.

The only studies in which this method has been applied to British penal measures in general have been those carried out by W. H. Hammond and others in the Home Office Research Unit.[8] In these studies the variables used to calculate expected rates have been hard data which appear to be closely associated with the probability of reconviction in all samples of offenders, that is, sex, age, type of offence and previous convictions.

Applying this technique to the known reconvictions within five years of some 27,000 male offenders of all ages from eight upwards, Hammond arrived at Table 17.

Interpreting Hammond

If Table 17 is taken at its face value, the penal measure which displays the greatest comparative efficacy in terms of reconvictions is fining, since the subsequent reconvictions were markedly and consistently below expectation both for first offenders and for recidivists.

In contrast, the percentages for imprisonment appear to support those who argue that it is not merely ineffective, but also detrimental. Here Hammond's separate analysis of Scottish first offender's subsequent careers is relevant, for it suggested that it is the sentences of less than six months of which this is true, while for longer sentences – that

8. See *The Sentence of the Court*, pt 6 (Home Office, 1969) and *Report on The Use of Short Sentences of Imprisonment by the Courts*, Appendix F (Scottish Advisory Council on the Treatment of Offenders, 1960).

Table 17
Actual Reconvictions as Percentages of Those Expected

Penal measure	Age-group and type of offender							
	under 17		17–20		21–9		30 and over	
	1st off-enders	Others	1st off-enders	Others	1st off-enders	Others	1st off-enders	Others
Discharge	89	100	89	98	109	90	133	104
Fines	75	83	75	94	63	99	84	65
Probation	118	101	122	101	153	115	(150)*	121
Approved school	138	102	—	—	—	—	—	—
Borstal	—	101	—	95	—	—	—	—
Detention centre	—	106	150†	110	—	—	—	—
Detention centre	—	119	—	—	—	—	—	—
Imprisonment	—	—	—	106‡	146§	111‡	(91)*§	104‡

* Percentages in brackets indicate that the numbers were very small.

† The number of juvenile first offenders in the sample who were committed to penal institutions of these kinds seems to have been too small to provide a satisfactory percentage; and for similar reasons the first offenders aged seventeen to twenty had to be combined for these penal institutions. The report says 'Of the group, the Borstal result was the best, being about average in effectiveness.'

‡ The calculation was based on a three-year instead of a five-year follow-up, and sentences of three years or more were excluded.

§ Six sentences of three years or more were excluded.

is, in most cases, sentences of six to twelve months – the reconviction rate was better than expected.

The percentages are disappointing for the advocates of probation. They are consistent with Wilkins's finding that in terms of reconvictions the efficacy of probation does not differ much from that of imprisonment. Worse still, it is in the case of first offenders that probation appears least effective. Here the possibility that courts are selecting the more difficult cases for probation must seriously be considered; but there are other possibilities which will be discussed later in this chapter. One minor observation of Hammond's is worth noting because it is so difficult to explain that if it had not occurred in all age groups it could have been dismissed as the product of chance. This was that although first offenders convicted of 'breaking and entering' had a high reconviction rate in comparison with other first offenders, for those put on probation it was lower than the reconviction rate for other first offenders on probation.

Equally interesting are the percentages for discharges. For young first offenders they are well below expectation, and may reflect (a) the spontaneous reform rate, (b) the absolute efficacy of the experience of mere detection and conviction or, in all probability, both. Even in the case of the older offender and the recidivist they are, with one exception, not markedly above expectation.

The exception is the older first offender: unless the high figure of 133 per cent is the product of chance (a possibility that can never be completely eliminated), it may reflect the probability that a first offender in his thirties, forties or fifties is a person who has committed several undetected offences, and has succumbed at last to the geometric progression of his chances of detection. In this situation he is unlikely to be impressed by a single experience of detection and conviction which does not involve a penalty. (See the discussion of 'immunity' on page 35.)

So far I have interpreted the figures by assuming that we can take them at their face value. Other possibilities, however, must be considered: and in particular the possibility that they reflect the courts' skill in choosing the right measures rather than the comparative efficacy of those measures. It is not inconceivable that sentencers were, by and large, choosing discharges and fines for offenders who seemed likely to go straight, and probation and imprisonment for those who did not; and that their diagnosis was correct more often than it would have been by chance. Against this are the awkward facts that sentencers are influenced by age, type of offence and criminal record; that these are strongly associated with the probability of reconviction; and that Hammond's table takes them into account. In other words, if we believe that the table reflects sentencers' skill rather than comparative efficacy we must be prepared to maintain that sentencers were able to weigh in their minds not only Hammond's three factors but also a number of subtler ones. Moreover, we must also maintain that the sentencers' main aim was to allot offenders to different measures according to their estimated probability of reconviction. It is highly improbable that sentencers are either so skilful in their calculation or so utilitarian in their aims. No doubt Table 17 reflects some skill in sentencing, for example, in identifying offenders who will go straight if merely discharged, but it is most unlikely that this is all that it reflects.

Deterred or Reformed?

A man who refrains from committing further offences after he has been subjected to some penal measure may do so because he wishes to avoid the same or a more severe penal measure in the future, because he now resists temptation from other motives or because he no longer feels temptation. Common sense and experience tell us that the last of these is a very rare transformation; we are entitled to assume that in all but the exceptional case the efficacy of a penal measure is attributable either to individual deterrence or to some more subtle process of learning to resist temptation to which I have applied the term 'reform' in an attempt to beg no questions as to its nature. Such evidence as there is suggests very strongly that both processes take place. It is highly unlikely that the after-effects of, say, six months spent in an overcrowded local prison can be anything more than a deterrent, just as it is highly unlikely that the influence of probation is mainly deterrent. The apparent efficacy of large fines is a tribute to the deterrent effect either of the fines themselves or in a few cases of imprisonment for non-payment. So much seems obvious. What is more interesting is the question whether a measure which cannot but be a deterrent can also be designed so that it has a reformative influence; for this is the direction in which the Prison Department, under the pressure of penal reformers, is trying to develop the prison system.

The question to be answered seems to be this: on the assumption that both measures which are primarily individual deterrents, and measures which are primarily reformative have some degree of absolute corrective efficacy, can the efficacy of the deterrent measure be increased by introducing into it features that are intended to reform? For example, can the reconviction rate after imprisonment be reduced by introducing a reformative régime into the prisons? The study which comes nearest to providing evidence on this question is Benson's comparison of the reconviction rates of male young prisoners after discharge from Lewes or Stafford prisons with those of youths of the same age range who had instead spent their sentence in Borstals (see Benson, 1959). The two groups were subdivided by means of the Mannheim–Wilkins prediction formula[9] into four categories, each with a different expectation of reconviction. Even so, there was no

9. This technique is explained on pages 132–3.

significant difference between the actual reconvictions, in any of the four categories, of those who had been in Borstal and those who had been in prison for roughly the same length of time. This comparison suffered from certain limitations. Although the ages of both young prisoners and Borstal youths ranged from sixteen to twenty-one on reception, 80 per cent of the young prisoners as compared with only 30 per cent of the Borstal youths, were over nineteen, and as we have seen the older an offender the lower his reconviction rate is likely to be. Secondly, the Borstal régime at this early post-war period had not developed some of its present features such as group counselling.

Nevertheless there can be no doubt that the Borstal régime of those days was intended to differ, and did differ, from the prison régime in ways that were meant to make it more than a pure deterrent. 'The objects of training,' said the Borstal Rules, 'shall be to bring to bear every influence which may establish in the inmates the will to lead a good and useful life on release, and to fit them to do so by the fullest possible development of their character, capacities and sense of personal responsibility.' Staff were specially selected with this end in mind, and there is no doubt that the majority of them were – and are – making a genuine effort to achieve them. Unless, therefore, Benson's comparison is to be dismissed completely – and its limitations are scarcely serious enough to justify that – they must be interpreted in one of two ways. Either Borstal and prison are equally effective individual deterrents for males of this age range, in which case the effort to supplement the deterrent effect by a process of socialization was unsuccessful; or else Borstals deterred a smaller percentage of their inmates than did prisons, but made up for this by socializing some of the others. The latter hypothesis is the more encouraging, but it involves one slightly improbable supposition which must now be discussed.

Mis-Classification

At one or two points in these discussions of the evidence for absolute or comparative corrective efficacy I have side-stepped a possibility to which attention was drawn some time ago by a Californian experiment. This possibility is that studies in which known reconviction rates of samples of offenders do not differ significantly after the application of different kinds of penal measure, are simply reflecting the defects of our present methods of allocating offenders to these different measures. An experiment in the institutional treatment of adult male delinquents from the United States Navy and Marines was reported by Grant and Grant (1959). At Camp Elliott, 511 of these delinquents were divided into groups of twenty, each of which was confined for six to nine weeks with three volunteer non-commissioned officers from the Marines and a psychologist consultant. Communication between delinquents and persons outside these groups was kept to a minimum. Treatment took the form of group discussions on five days a week, and also constant, unrelieved contact with other members of the group (and with supervisors, two out of three being on duty every day). 'Success' was judged by subsequent careers on restoration to duty, although unfortunately the criteria and follow-up period are not described in the published reports. It was found that delinquents classified as of 'high maturity' did better after being in some groups than in others, and so did those of 'low maturity'. But the two groups which seemed to have the best effect on the 'mature' men appeared to have least success with the 'immature men'; two other groups seemed to achieve much the same success with either type, on a level intermediate between the high success rate of the immature men under the first two régimes. The difference seemed to lie in the personality types of the supervisors. The interest of the study lay not in what it proved but in what it suggested, namely that a type of treatment which has a high comparative efficacy when applied to individuals of one psychological type may actually have a below average efficacy when applied to another type. In loose terms, which ignore the fact that we cannot estimate absolute efficacy, what does a mature man good may do an immature man harm.

This possibility is obviously very relevant to the interpretation of studies in which penal measures that are obviously different in nature – such as prison and probation – appear to have roughly equal comparative efficacy. An imaginary example will illustrate the possibilities. Let us suppose that in a group of 220 offenders all the ninety first offenders are put on probation, while the 130 with previous convictions are imprisoned; and that a three-year follow-up discloses very similar reconviction rates of 50 per cent and 49 per cent respectively. The hypothesis is that each of the subgroups is a mixture of men of at least two psychological types (A and B) of which one has a low reconviction rate after probation, but a high rate after imprisonment, and vice versa (see Table 18).

Table 18
The Mis-Classification Hypothesis Illustrated

Penal measure	Psychological type	N	Known 3-year reconvictions	Apparent reconviction rate
Prison	A	60	15 (=25%)	49%
	B	70	49 (=70%)	
Probation	A	40	26 (=65%)	50%
	B	50	19 (=38%)	

Clearly, if all offenders of type A had been allocated to prison, while all those of type B had been put on probation, the reconviction rates of each group might well have been lower. If so, we would have been employing a more relevant criterion for classification.

Less obvious is the possibility that what is regarded as a single method of treatment should really be subdivided into two or more categories. For instance, it is possible that men placed on probation are being allocated to a variety of supervisors, in such a way that some are going to supervisors who reduce their chance of reconviction, some to supervisors who increase it, but who would reduce the chance of reconviction of another type of probationer; and that if this were remedied by relevant classification the comparative efficacy of probation would rise above that of prison. Correspondingly, it might be possible to raise the comparative efficacy of prison or Borstal in the same way.

Interchangeability of Penal Measures

On the other hand it is premature to assume, as so many discussions of sentencing policy do, that for all or most offenders there is a single correct choice of sentence surrounded by wrong choices, and to insist that sentencing should invariably be preceded by diagnosis for this reason. The fallacy lies not merely in the assumption that our limited and not very sophisticated repertoire of penalties must include one that is effective in each case. Consider what is logically possible in the

120   Measuring Corrective Efficacy

case of an offender who appears before a sentencer. He may belong to one of a number of groups:

1. Those who will go straight whatever the sentence.

2. Those who will not go straight whatever the sentence.

3. Those who will go straight if given a certain sentence but not any of the others.

4. Those who will go straight if given one of two sentences, but not the others.

5. Those who will go straight if given one of three sentences, and so on, until the group is reached for whom there is only one ineffective sentence.

We have no information at present from which we can estimate the relative sizes of these groups, or indeed can be certain that some of them exist at all. We can infer from the existence of recidivists with long penal records that there is a group (2) for whom none of the sentencer's present choices is effective.[10] Again, it seems probable, from the encouraging results of nominal measures such as discharge, that there is a group (1) of offenders who will go straight whatever measure is applied.[11] It is the existence of the other groups, for which the choice of sentence makes a difference, that is more problematical. The fact that some offenders are reconvicted after being fined, but not after a subsequent prison sentence, suggests that prison would have been a better choice on the first occasion. But it is possible that their personality or circumstances changed in the interval,[12] and even if they did not we cannot infer that prison was the only correct choice.

What must be emphasized is that there is as yet no empirical evidence which points conclusively, or even persuasively, to the existence of a large number of offenders for whom on any given occasion the

10. The alternative explanation, that between each successive attempt to correct the recidivist by fines, probation and imprisonment his personality or circumstances change so that choices which would have been effective at other times happen to be ineffective on that occasion, is too implausible.

11. No doubt some who go straight after being discharged would not go straight if subjected to some penalty which they considered excessive, such as prison. But to grant this is not to abolish group 1.

12. This is not as implausible as the superficially similar hypothesis in note 10 above.

sentencer has open to him one and only one effective choice. The common assumption that most offenders fall into this group, and that the right choice can be discovered by a process of diagnosis before sentence, is probably the result of thinking of penal treatment as analogous to medical or psychiatric treatment, or more precisely to an idealized version of it in which diagnosis invariably precedes and points unerringly to the remedy. The dangers of this analogy are discussed more fully in Walker (1969, chs. 7 and 8, and Appendix A).

Chapter 14
Predictive Techniques

So far as penologists are concerned, predictive techniques have three distinguishable uses, each with its own set of problems. The first is the estimation of the probability that a member of a not-yet-delinquent sample of people will become delinquent in the future: the classic example is the Gluecks' (1950) formula for 'predicting' future delinquency among boys. The second is the estimation of the probability that a member of a sample of known offenders will offend again in the future or, more precisely, will be detected again in an offence: the classic, though not the earliest, example is Mannheim and Wilkins's (1955) formula for 'predicting' reconviction among released Borstal boys. To distinguish these two uses I shall call them 'onset prediction' and 'relapse prediction'. The third use will be described later. What onset and relapse prediction have in common is that they are intended as aids to decision-making in a situation of a special kind, that is, in which for one reason or another it is desirable to separate a population into at least two groups, which will be differently treated.

For example, we are nowadays sufficiently deterministic to agree that certain children are more likely than others to develop into delinquents, although our explanations may be so complex and speculative as to be almost useless for preventive purposes. Since our resources for helping such children are so limited that they cannot be offered to them all, it is rational to look for the most accurate way of identifying likely future delinquents so that these resources can be applied to them. Similarly, if the pressure on prison or Borstal accommodation is so great that some men must be released at an earlier stage of their sentences than others, it is rational to seek the most accurate way of distinguishing prisoners or Borstal trainees with high and low probabilities of recidivism.

Coping with Uncertainty

It is important to realize that we can hardly ever base this distinction on certainty. Occasionally we may come across a case in which a known offender is virtually certain not to repeat his offence. An example is the infanticidal mother who is now past child-bearing age. But normally we can talk only of probabilities. It is also important to appreciate what this means. To say that a prisoner has a 20 per cent probability of reconviction means nothing more than that, on the information which we have about him and other prisoners, we have assigned him to a subgroup of which, on our experience of past samples, we expect 20 per cent to be reconvicted. Note, too, that we are seldom able to state with certainty that 20 per cent of the subgroup will be reconvicted. In certain situations we could do so: for instance, if we knew that the police intended, and would be able, to arrange the conviction of one in every five of the subgroup. But such situations do not arise in penology.[1]

Consequently, two sorts of uncertainty are involved. One is whether the individual will fall into the minority who will be reconvicted or into the majority who will not. The other is whether the minority and the majority will in fact have the same relative sizes as our experience of past samples suggests. The second sort of uncertainty can be reduced, though never entirely excluded, by detecting and eliminating sources of bias in the sample, by increasing its size and by ensuring that it is as recent a sample as possible. (It was found, for example, that the accuracy of the Mannheim–Wilkins formula, which was based on the reconvictions of a 1946–7 sample of Borstal boys, declined progressively when applied to later samples, presumably because of changing chances of detection and other environmental factors.)

The first sort of uncertainty can be reduced only by increasing the relevant information or improving one's mathematical technique for making use of it. Thus one might begin by being able to subdivide prisoners into only two subgroups, one with an 80 per cent reconviction rate, the other with a 30 per cent rate. Improved information or techniques might make it possible to split them instead into three

1. They do arise in other fields, however: for example, if we know that, say, ten prizes are to be distributed amongst 1000 ticket-holders in a lottery.

124   Predictive Techniques

groups, one with a 90 per cent rate, one with a 60 per cent rate and one with a 25 per cent rate. If so, one would have more confidence in treating members of the first group on the assumption that they would be reconvicted, and members of the third on the assumption that they would not. But even if one ended up with a subgroup whose reconviction rate was zero or 100 per cent one would not have removed the second sort of uncertainty, which is inseparable from sampling.

A simple example will illustrate these points. If we have, for some practical purpose such as parole, to distinguish between prisoners with high and low probabilities of reconviction within, say, three years of release we might begin by taking a sample of prisoners released in 1965, and subdivide them according to what is called the 'criterion variable': that is, into those which were and those which were not so reconvicted (see Table 19).

Table 19
Twenty Imaginary Prisoners

		Scores	
Reconvicted		*A*	*B*
0001	young, unmarried, unemployed, first offender	3	2
0002	young, married, unemployed, first offender	2	1
0005	middle-aged, divorced, employed, previous conviction	2	2
0009	elderly, married, unemployed, first offender	1	1
0013	young, married, unemployed, previous convictions	3	2
0014	middle-aged, married, unemployed, first offender	1	1
0019	young, unmarried, unemployed, previous convictions	4	3
Not reconvicted			
0003	young, married, employed, first offender	1	—
0004	middle-aged, married, unemployed, first offender	1	1
0006	elderly, unmarried, employed, first offender	1	1
0007	middle-aged, married, unemployed, first offender	1	1
0008	young, unmarried, employed, first offender	2	1
0010	middle-aged, married, employed, first offender	—	—
0011	young, married, unemployed, first offender	2	1
0012	young, married, employed, previous convictions	2	1
0015	elderly, married, employed, first offender	—	—
0016	middle-aged, married, employed, previous convictions	1	1
0017	young, unmarried, employed, first offender	2	1
0018	middle-aged, unmarried, employed, first offender	1	1
0020	young, married, unemployed, previous convictions	3	2

We should then collect as many items of information about each prisoner as his dossier and our resources allowed. Let us assume, in order to make the example manageable, that our sample is limited to twenty prisoners and our recorded information to their age, marital status, employment when sentenced, and previous criminal record. (These have been shown in the example above in a way that is designed for simplicity rather than accuracy.) We are then in a position to construct a formula for predicting reconviction. A simple process of counting shows that:

Of the reconvicted	Of the unreconvicted	
57%	46%	were young
43%	23%	were not married
86%	39%	were unemployed
43%	23%	had previous convictions

Clearly, being young, unmarried, unemployed and having a bad record are all associated with being reconvicted. The simplest kind of prediction formula – the kind which was originally used – would award a score to each prisoner by giving one mark for being young, one for being unmarried, one for being unemployed and one for previous convictions (as has been done in column A). The result would be:

Score	Number of prisoners with score	Number reconvicted	Reconviction rate
4	1	1	100%
3	3	2	67%
2	6	2	33%
1	8	2	25%
0	2	—	0%

Thus, it would be rational to proceed with our decision-making on the assumption that prisoners with a score of 4 or 3 would be reconvicted, but that those with lower scores would not. If future samples behaved like this one, this assumption would be right in fifteen out of twenty cases, but wrong in five (for one prisoner would be wrongly classified as due to be reconvicted, and four as due not to be). We could improve on this, however. For example, the attribute 'being young' is not very strongly associated with reconviction; and if we disregard it

126 Predictive Techniques

we would have a system of scoring with a maximum of three points (shown in column B) which, as it happens, could be applied so as to give rise to only *four* mistaken classifications: three prisoners with a score of 1 would be wrongly treated as not due to be reconvicted, and one prisoner with a score of 2 would be wrongly treated as due to be reconvicted.

Validating the Formula

It must be realized that all we have by this stage is an untried prediction formula. It cannot be regarded as useful until it has been 'validated' – that is, tried out on a sample other than the one from which it was constructed. After all, the twenty prisoners on which this particular formula has been based may be grossly unrepresentative of the population on which the formula is intended for use, although in practice we would have taken a much larger sample, and taken precautions against avoidable bias. So a validating sample must be collected, and the formula used to see how well it discriminates between prisoners who are subsequently reconvicted and prisoners who are not. It should discriminate almost as well (i.e. lead to about the same number of mistakes) amongst the validating sample as amongst the construction sample, if both are good samples from the same population. We must not expect it to discriminate quite as well, because it has been devised to fit as closely as possible to a single sample, which almost certainly was not exactly representative of the population from which it was drawn, while the second sample must also be slightly unrepresentative, and almost certainly in slightly different ways.[2]

Ideally, there should be more than one validating sample: the first being drawn from the same 'cohort' of prisoners as the construction sample (that is, from prisoners released during the same period), and others from later cohorts. For experience has shown that the longer the period that elapses between the construction and use of a prediction formula the less well it is likely to discriminate, although it is unlikely to lose its power of discrimination altogether. Therefore the first validating sample should be taken so as to show how well the formula discriminates under optimum conditions – more precisely,

2. In fact, the Mannheim–Wilkins formula did slightly *better* with its validating sample than with the construction sample, but this must have been sheer luck.

when applied to samples known to be from the same population as the construction sample; the later ones to see whether its power of discrimination is declining sufficiently to suggest that the nature of the population, or outside conditions after its release, have changed (in which case the formula will have to be brought up to date).

One more point: knowledge of the way in which the data have been collected and used, always desirable, is doubly so when prediction formulae are being applied in practice. To take a crude example in Table 19, if one is going to apply the scoring system to a new group of parolees one must know what was counted as a 'first offence' in compiling that table. Were previous convictions for non-indictable offences disregarded or not? Again, was a man classified as 'unmarried' if he was divorced, or merely cohabiting?

As for methods of constructing the formula, information is seldom as simple as in Table 19, and more complex methods of scoring have been developed which give different weight to different attributes according to the strength of their association with the criterion variable. Again, the Mannheim–Wilkins formula is an example. A different method is called 'predictive attribute analysis' and is very clearly explained and illustrated by Grygier (1966, pp. 279 ff). We need not be concerned, however, with the technical refinements of predictive methods. It is more important to be clear about several points which apply to all methods.

Misgivings

In the first place, some people have misgivings about the use of arithmetic as a basis for arriving at decisions which affect the lives of human beings. Their objections need careful analysis before they can be dismissed. It is perfectly legitimate to argue:

1. That one should never allow oneself to be in a position in which one has to discriminate for penal purposes between people on the basis of mere probabilities as regards their future conduct. This is an ethical argument which must be respected, however impractical it may be. It would, of course, involve either abandoning such practices as parole, or using them in a strictly retributive way (parole, for instance, could be granted as a reward for good conduct, or with regard to the heinousness of the offender's record). But it is not a completely illogical argument.

128 Predictive Techniques

2. That it is dangerous to make predictions about future law-breaking (or indeed any kind of social failure) if these involve 'labelling' certain people as prospective failures. If people know that they have been labelled in this way the label may cause them to fail, so that the prediction will be self-fulfilling, and therefore pernicious. Even if the subjects do not know that they have been labelled as likely failures (and this is hard to prevent) the label may have the same indirect effect – although a weaker one no doubt – by altering the attitudes of penal agents, such as probation and after-care officers, towards them. The worst that can be said about this argument is that, in the penal field at least, the evidence in support of it is scanty and susceptible to other interpretations. What is less tenable is the argument:

3. That while one is entitled to base penal decisions on beliefs about people's future conduct, these beliefs should not be arrived at by arithmetic. This argument sometimes takes the extreme form of asserting that one can predict other people's future conduct more accurately on the basis of one's personal reaction to them. In a more realistic form it admits that prediction is helped by using information about them, but asserts that it is better (i.e. more accurate) if the information is not used arithmetically. This has been called the 'clinical' approach, as distinct from the 'actuarial' one, which assumes the contrary.

On the whole both evidence and logic are against this argument (for an excellent review of the clinical and actuarial ideologies, see Meehl, 1954). The implausibility of the purely clinical approach should be clear to anyone who tried to use Table 19 *without counting* in order to see what information distinguished reconvicted from unreconvicted prisoners. 'Impressionism' makes rather poor use of even a mildly complex collection of facts such as this.

What I am not arguing about is that predictions should dispense with information gained from personal contact with the subjects. In this imaginary example personally acquired knowledge of the prisoners might have improved the accuracy of the prediction in several ways. It might have discovered that 'having a job to go to' was a much better predictor of success than any of those in the table. Or it might have shown that 'having previous convictions' could be made into a much better predictor by distinguishing convictions for dishonesty from other sorts. Or (though this is unlikely) that men who said they were going to go straight did so, while those who were doubtful failed.

When to Disregard the Formula

Nor am I arguing that actuarial predictions should never be disregarded in the light of other knowledge about the subjects. From this point of view, however, it is essential to distinguish:

1. Information which is *used* in the prediction formula. It would obviously be illogical, for example, to take prisoner 0013 out of the 'likely to be reconvicted' group simply because one believed that married men were unlikely to be reconvicted, for the prediction formula takes account of this, and still places him amongst those likely to be reconvicted.

2. Information which was *considered and discarded* in constructing the formula. In our example, since the formula was not weakened – but in this case actually improved slightly – by omitting the attribute 'youth', it would be illogical to take prisoner 0003 out of the 'unlikely to be reconvicted' group simply because he was young.

3. Information about attributes which are known or likely to be *closely associated* with attributes in group 1 or 2: for example, about national insurance contributions, which are closely linked to employment. It would be rational to see whether the formula could be made more accurate by substituting this attribute, but quite irrational to use it as a basis for overruling the formula.

4. Information which was *not* considered in constructing the formula. In certain circumstances it would be justifiable to disregard the result of using a prediction formula in the light of such information. Some information which is most unlikely to be available to constructors of prediction formulae might be extremely relevant. For example, although prisoner 0015 obviously belongs to the 'unlikely to be reconvicted' group, one would be justified in ignoring this if one were told that while in prison he had been persuaded by prisoner 0019 to join him in a planned robbery after their release. Some attributes, though very relevant, are so rare that they are unusable in a general formula. If one knew that prisoner 0019 had suffered an accident which confined him to a wheel-chair one would be justified in removing him from the high-risk group.

Common sense should be a reliable guide in deciding when one is justified in disregarding prediction formulae. Even common sense, however, may be seduced by information of type 4 which is unquantifiable, or stated in an unquantifiable way. One may be told by a penal agent who has been in close contact with the prisoner that 'Whatever the actuarial probabilities, there's something about him that makes us feel he is going to get into trouble again.' Often such 'hunches' appear to be confirmed with impressive frequency simply because the group of offenders in question has a very high reconviction rate. Someone who invariably predicted reconviction for men released from long preventive sentences would be right four times out of five, and might easily acquire a spurious reputation for clinical skill.

Choosing a Cut-Off Point

A problem of a different sort concerns what is called the 'cut-off point'. In column B in Table 19, we could 'cut off' the 'likely to be reconvicted group' just below three points, in which case only prisoners like 0019 would be assigned to it. This would minimize the number of mistaken assignments to this group, but would result in a lot of mistaken assignments to the 'unlikely to be reconvicted' group. At the other extreme we could assign only prisoners with a score of zero to the 'unlikely' group which would minimize mistaken assignments to that group, but result in a lot of mistaken assignments to the other group. If all we care about is minimizing the number of mistakes *of either kind*, the best cut-off point is between scores of 2 and 1, which results in only four mistakes. But three of these mistakes consist of wrongly assigning prisoners to the high-risk group. If the consequences of being classified as 'likely to be reconvicted' were very serious for the prisoner or very demanding on scarce resources (as a long delay in parole might be) we might decide that this was not the optimum cut-off point, and that we would prefer one which minimized not the *total* number of mistakes, but the number of mistakes *of this kind*.

Prediction and Parole

Examples of the actual use of prediction in the British penal system are rare. Its most important use is to be found in the parole procedure.

Normally, to be released on parole before his due date a prisoner must:

1. Be eligible under the terms of the statute, that is, have served one year or one-third of his sentence, whichever is the longer.

2. Have consented to be considered for parole (some do not).

3. Be recommended for it by the Local Review Committee for his prison.

4. Be recommended for it by the National Parole Board, who are told what his predicted chances of reconviction are within two years of release.

The variation between the characteristics of different prison populations means that Local Review Committees tend to set different standards in recommending parole. The Home Office Research Unit, therefore, calculates the reconviction probability of every prisoner who is eligible for parole, and if it turns out to be less than a cut-off point, which is at present 36 per cent, he is put forward for consideration by the Parole Board even if he is not recommended by the Local Review Committee. In about three-quarters of such cases the Parole Board agrees with the Local Review Committee, but tends to recommend the release of roughly one-quarter. The main characteristics used in the formula are prisoners' criminal, penal and employment records.[3]

Base Expectancies

Finally, as I said at the beginning of this chapter, there is a use for predictive methods which is not directly designed for decision-making. One way of assessing the comparative corrective efficacy of different penal measures is, as we have seen, to use relevant variables to work out an 'expected' reconviction rate for those subjected to each measure, and then compare this with the actual rate. This can be done either in the way illustrated in Chapter 13, or simply by grouping one's sample of offenders into different probability groups, according to their likelihood of reconviction, as is done in ordinary prediction exercises. Each probability group is then subdivided into those subjected to each penal measure, and the actual reconviction rates are

3. See the *Annual Report of the Parole Board for 1969* (Parole Board, 1970).

studied to see whether they differ for different measures. The method thus consists, in a sense, of matching groups subjected to different measures according to each group's expected reconviction rate: it could therefore be called 'matching by prediction'. The classic example is Mannheim and Wilkins's use of their probability groups to compare the reconviction rates of Borstal boys from 'open' and 'closed' Borstals (see Table 20).

Table 20
Percentage of Borstal Boys not Convicted within Three and a Half Years after Leaving

Probability of relapse	Open Borstals		Closed Borstals	
	long stays	short stays	long stays	short stays
Low-risk group	60	86	67	67
Intermediate group	55	67	58	54
High-risk group	40	37	27	30

Table 20 shows that both high-risk and low-risk boys – as well as those in the intermediate group – did better after a stay in an open Borstal, and preferably a short stay. As in the case of Table 17 in Chapter 13, however, we cannot entirely rule out the possibility that this table reflects the skill of Borstal allocation centres in selecting the better boys for the open Borstals; but at that date methods of allocation were primitive and this is unlikely.

'Matching by prediction' is extensively used in some penal systems – notably in California – for assessing the effectiveness of different forms of penal treatment. Offenders are assigned a 'base expectancy rate', calculated from past reconviction rates of offenders with similar attributes, that is, each offender's attributes are used to assign him to a probability group. If a sufficient sample of offenders subjected to a given penal treatment yields fewer reconvictions than its base expectancy rates would predict, this is taken as an indication that the treatment is effective.

Epilogue

The reader who has reached this part of the book should be able not only to make use of officially published criminal statistics but also to follow the arguments of criminological research workers, at least to the extent of understanding what it is that they are trying to do with their figures. He may not be able to appreciate or criticize the mathematical techniques which they have adopted, so that he may have to stay on the touch-line so far as some controversies are concerned. For example, in 1960 L. T. Wilkins published a report called 'Delinquent generations', in which he analysed the conviction rates of successive cohorts of British children as they grew up. His analysis led to the conclusion that children whose fourth or fifth year of life fell within the period of the 1939–45 war (or the depression of the early 1930s) were particularly prone to be found guilty of indictable offences. This conclusion has been attacked, however, by Rose (1968), who argued that Wilkins's method was bound to create an 'artificial delinquent generation', which might well be a complete illusion. The controversy continues.

More commonly, however, it is the data rather than the technique of analysis which repays a critical examination; and here the layman may notice what the sophisticated statistician has overlooked. For example, one elaborate study of the reconvictions of a group of prisoners turned out, on close reading, to be based on follow-up periods which varied from three and a half to ten months.

Nevertheless, the non-mathematical user of criminal statistics may occasionally find himself in need of a little expertise. If so, he can of course consult the text books; and certainly one learns most from them when one has a specific problem. On the other hand, it may take him some little time to find a section which is relevant to his difficulty. He would, for example, have to search hard to find a thorough discussion of the problem which is dealt with on pages 52–7 of this book. Again, he may be misled into employing an unsuitable technique. Suppose that he is looking for a significance test (see Chapter 11) to tell him how much weight to attach to differences between two matched samples. Most textbooks will offer him the chi-square test, without warning him that it is inappropriate for matched pairs. If possible he should consult a statistician to make sure that he is on the right track.

Appendix A
Glossary of Technical Terms

assault 'Any act which intentionally or possibly recklessly causes another to apprehend immediate and unlawful personal violence' (*Fagan* v. *Commissioner of Metropolitan Police*: [1968] 2 All England Reports at 442). The term is often used, however, to include also a 'battery', which is 'the actual intended use of unlawful force to another without his consent' (ibid.).

bias A defect in the procedure for selecting a sample (q.v.) which ensures that certain subgroups of the population (q.v.) will be over-represented (q.v.).

buggery Sexual intercourse by the anus with a man or woman, or intercourse (by man or woman) with an animal by anus or vagina.

burglary Entering a building as a trespasser and with intent to commit theft, grievous bodily harm, rape or unlawful damage; or committing or attempting theft or grievous bodily harm after entering a building as a trespasser. Now statutorily defined in section 9 of the Theft Act 1968, the term was previously restricted to breaking and entering dwellings at night with intent to commit a felony.

caution (a) An interview or letter in which the police tell an offender that he is merely being warned and not prosecuted on this occasion (sometimes called a 'police warning').
(b) A warning which Judges' Rules require the police to give at a certain stage to a suspect whom they are questioning.

child In English criminal law, a person under fourteen years of age (see also 'young person').

clear-up percentage The percentage of offences recorded by police which is traced to offenders with sufficient evidence to justify a prosecution (even if one does not result); but see Chapter 3.

cohort A group selected for follow-up so that it includes all the persons born (or sentenced, or released from custody, and so on, as the case may be) between certain dates; less precisely, a sample from such a group.

control sample One selected so that its members differ from that of the 'experimental' sample in respect of the variable which is being investigated, e.g. have not received the treatment whose efficacy is being assessed. It may or may not be matched (q.v.) to the experimental sample.

daily average population The average number of different individuals in a residential establishment or class of such establishments.

dark figure The amount of crime, or of a given type of crime, which is not reported to law enforcement agencies.

dependent variable The variable whose causal or statistical dependence on other variables (the 'independent variables') is being studied.

expectancy An individual's probability of a future contingency (such as reconviction) calculated from the experience of a sample of individuals with similar characteristics. For 'base expectancy rates' see page 132.

first offender An offender who is found guilty of an offence for the first time (in the First Offenders Act 1958, an offender convicted for the first time since his seventeenth birthday of an indictable offence).

grievous bodily harm 'Really serious' bodily harm to a human being (*D.P.P.* v. *Smith*: [1961] A.C.290 at p. 334).

gross indecency between males Although neither statute nor case law provides a clear definition, it appears to mean a sexual act between males, not amounting to buggery (q.v.).

hybrid offence One which is indictable (q.v.) in certain circumstances but otherwise non-indictable (q.v.).

immunity In criminology, the probability of committing an offence, or series of offences, without being identified as the offender by a law enforcement agency.

imprisonable (*offence*) A clumsy but convenient word to indicate an offence for which an adult can be sentenced to imprisonment.

incidence The frequency of occurrences of a given phenomenon in a given period (e.g. the annual incidence of attacks of influenza): to be distinguished from prevalence (q.v.).

indecent assault Although neither statute nor case law provides a clear definition, it seems to be an assault 'accompanied by circumstances of indecency' on the offender's part (see Archbold, section 2981) but not amounting to rape, buggery or attempts thereat. Assault (q.v.) does not necessarily involve physical contact although the charge is hardly ever brought if this has not taken place.

independent variable See 'dependent variable'.

index (a) A series of artificial numbers which enable more than one variable to be combined for the purpose of enabling periods, areas, periods of time, etc. to be compared easily in respect of one or more variables, e.g. a 'cost-of-living index'.

(b) A method of keeping records of persons, incidents, etc. (e.g. on cards) which enables the record for a given individual to be inserted or removed, e.g. the Home Office's Offenders' Index.

indictable (*offence*) One which either must or may in certain circumstances be tried on indictment, i.e. before a jury at Assizes, a Crown Court or Quarter Sessions; and see 'non-indictable'.

judicial statistics Figures showing trials and their results. Judicial statistics may be 'civil' or 'criminal'.

juvenile A convenient, but non-legal term for a person who is either a child (q.v.) or a young person (q.v.); see 'juvenile court'.

juvenile court A specially constituted magistrates' court with jurisdiction over juveniles, except those charged with offences which must be tried on indictment.

matching The process of ensuring that a control group resembles the sample under study in respect of one or more relevant variables.

moving average An average calculated from two or more consecutive numbers in a series. Thus in a series of annual figures the moving three-year average for a given year is the average of the figures for the three years of which the given year is the second.

non-indictable (*offence*) One which may be tried only by a summary court, i.e. a magistrates' court; but see hybrid offences.

over-represented More frequent in a sample than in the population (q.v.). Thus children are over-represented in the audience at circuses.

population (or *universe*) The class of people or things which is being studied by taking a sample (q.v.).

prediction In criminology, the use of characteristics associated with the commission of offences (such as poor employment record) to subdivide collections of individuals into groups with different probabilities of this.

prevalence The number of individuals exhibiting a characteristic, e.g. alcoholism, at a given point of time ('point prevalence') or over a short period of time ('period prevalence'). To be distinguished from incidence (q.v.) thus: in a population of a hundred the prevalence of influenza could never exceed a hundred, but its incidence could if the period were long enough to allow some members of the population to incur more than one bout of influenza.

principal offence The offence by which the offender is classified in Tables I or II of the *Criminal Statistics*. The Home Office rule for identifying the principal offence is explained on page 45.

quantitative (*data*) Divisible into groups distinguished by some quantity, e.g. houses of 1000 square feet, 1100 square feet, etc.

quasi-indicatable (*offence*) One which, though strictly non-indictable (q.v.), so closely resembles some group of indictable offences (q.v.) that it is treated as indictable when recording an offender's convictions. An example is indecent exposure, which is recorded along with indictable sexual offences.

random (*sample*) Chosen in such a way that each individual has the same chance of selection.

rate A number expressed as a fraction of the population at risk, e.g. '1 in 6', or '0·2 per million'. The commonest form of rate is a percentage.

reception Occasion on which an offender is received into a residential establishment, such as a prison. In annual reception statistics the same individual may be involved in more than one reception.

recidivist An offender who offends again after being sentenced. The term is often reserved, however, for offenders with lengthy criminal records ('multiple recidivists'), those with only one reconviction being known as 'primary recidivists'.

reconviction (*in studies of the effectiveness of sentences*) An occasion on which a sentenced offender is subsequently found guilty of a further offence or offences.

reportability (*of an offence*) The extent to which an offence is likely to be brought to the notice of an agency of law enforcement: sometimes called 'visibility'.

robbery Stealing by using force on a person or seeking to put them in fear of force. It is now statutorily defined in section 8 of the Theft Act 1968.

sample A group selected as representative of a population (q.v.) or 'universe', as a basis for inferences about the members of that population.

sampling frame A source of information about a population from which a sample can be drawn, e.g. an electoral register.

sampling procedure The rule(s) for selecting members of a sample (q.v.) from the sampling frame (q.v.), e.g. (a) take every tenth name from the electoral register, (b) when this leads to a person who cannot be interviewed, take the next name on the register.

significance A difference between rates is said to be 'significant' if the probability that it has occurred solely through the chance operation of sampling is low. This probability is calculated by one of a number of 'significance tests' (according to the nature of the data) and the result is expressed as a value of p (for probability).

standard list (offence) In the Home Office's *Instructions for the Preparation of Statistics Relating to Crime* (1964), a list of types of offence which must be included by police forces in their periodic reports of 'offences made known to the police'. Offences not on the standard list are recorded only in reports of prosecutions or cautions. All indictable offences and a few non-indictable offences are on the standard list.

stratified sample A sample (q.v.) which consists of subsamples selected so as to ensure that subdivisions of a population are represented.

taking into consideration (t.i.c.) A procedure by which an offender who has been convicted and is about to be sentenced can protect himself against subsequent prosecution and sentence for other offences of a similar kind by inviting the court to bear them in mind when sentencing him on this occasion.

universe See 'population'.

weighting Assigning different values to, e.g., different events, in a systematic way, e.g. in an index (q.v.) of seriousness of crime an assault might be given a weight of 10 and a theft a weight of 3.

wound To break the continuity of the whole skin (*Moriarty* v. *Brooks*: (1834) 6 C. & P., 684).

young person In English criminal law, a person between his fourteenth and seventeenth birthdays (see also 'child').

Appendix B
Main Sources of English Criminal Statistics

The main sources of periodical criminal, judicial and penal statistics which, unless otherwise indicated, are compiled *annually*.

Published By Her Majesty's Stationery Office

Criminal Statistics, England and Wales, from 1857 (judicial statistics from 1837).

Report of the Prison Commissioners (or, from 1963, Prison Department of the Home Office. From 1962 the main statistical tables have been published in a separate volume.)

Offences of Drunkenness (excluding those involving vehicles), from 1950. (Previously included in the *Licensing Statistics.*)

Offences Relating to Motor Vehicles, from 1928.

Statistics Relating to Approved Schools, Remand Homes and Attendance Centres in England and Wales, from 1962.

Report on the Work of the Children's Department (of the Home Office). (Nine have been published, at irregular intervals, from 1923.)

Report on the Work of the Probation and After-Care Department (of the Home Office). (Two have been published, one for 1962–5, one for 1966–8.)

Home Office Studies in the Causes of Delinquency and the Treatment of Offenders (at irregular intervals). Especially:
   No. 3 'Delinquent Generations',
   No. 4 'Murder',
   No. 8 'Trends and Regional Comparisons in Probation',
   No. 11 'Studies of Female Offenders'.

Home Office Research Studies, especially No. 3, 'Murder 1957 to 1968'.

Report of H.M. Inspectors of Constabulary, from 1945.

Unpublished, but Obtainable by Research Workers from the Home Office's Statistical Division

Supplementary Criminal Statistics, from 1949. (Some information, e.g. for separate police districts, which used to appear in the main volumes for previous years, is now in this series.)
Approved School Statistics, from 1956.
Approved School After-Care Statistics, from 1956.
Attendance Centre Index Statistics, from 1962.
Detention Centre Index Statistics, from 1961.
Borstal Index Statistics, from 1961.

Other Sources (Including Local Sources)

Report of the Metropolitan Police Commissioners (HMSO), from 1869.
Reports of Chief Constables.
Reports of Probation Committees.
Reports of Children's Departments.

Special Studies

Cambridge Department of Criminal Science, *Sexual Offences*, Macmillan, 1957.
F. H. McClintock and N. H. Avison, *Crime in England and Wales*, Heinemann, 1968.
F. H. McClintock, N. H. Avison, N. C. Savill, and V. L. Worthington, *Crimes of Violence*, Macmillan, 1963.
F. H. McClintock and E. Gibson, *Robbery in London*, Macmillan, 1961.
G. Rose, *The Struggle for Penal Reform*, Stevens, 1960. Appendix 1 summarizes the criminal statistics for quinquennia from 1857 to 1959.

Appendix C
The Perks Report

The Departmental Committee on Criminal Statistics, which has been referred to in this book as 'the Perks Committee', was appointed by the Home Secretary in 1963, under the Chairmanship of Mr Wilfred Perks, to overhaul the criminal statistics for England and Wales (a separate committee was appointed to deal with the Scottish criminal statistics, but came to very similar conclusions).

This was the second major overhaul of the English criminal statistics: the first took place in the 1890s. The Perks Report, published in 1967 as the *Report of the Departmental Committee on Criminal Statistics* (Cmnd.3448), made a large number of recommendations, which are summarized in its own words below. The cost of implementing them, however, in terms of both money and police man-hours, seems likely to be considerable, and so far none of the major ones have been carried out. Nevertheless it is to be hoped that during the 1970s there will be successive improvements on the lines proposed.

Summary of the Committee's Recommendations

(*a*) The revision of the system of classifying offences to give a more realistic grouping of similar offences than at present (paragraph 48(*b*) and (*c*)).

(*b*) The discouragement of the use of any single figure, and in particular the total number of recorded offences, as a general measure of the trend of crime, and the development of a set of indicators representing different kinds of offence (paragraphs 128 and 129).

(*c*) The adoption of a new Standard List of offences (including all indictable offences and certain other offences in categories regarded as sufficiently serious) for which information should be provided at the stage when the offence becomes known to the police (paragraph 48(*a*)).

(*d*) The collection of information about the circumstances of offences and characteristics of offenders (paragraphs 71 and 82).

(*e*) The revision of the rules for counting offences to deal more consistently and

144 Appendix C

logically with the problems created by multiple offences (events involving two or more classes of offence) and continuous or repetitive offences (paragraphs 55 to 59).

(f) The adoption by all police forces of a standard Crime Report form, incorporating all information needed either locally or nationally for statistical purposes and making provision for certain statistical coding and punching operations (paragraphs 68 to 80).

(g) The adaptation of standardized procedures for reporting the results of proceedings for Standard List offences to provide for linking the result of the case with the Crime Report form (paragraphs 48(f), 81 and 82).

(h) The decentralization to each police force of such part of the coding of data on forms and the production of the computer input medium (paper tape or cards) as may be found practicable, if the force concerned is willing to accept it in the interest of achieving a rapid feedback of information to it from a central computer (paragraphs 88 to 93).

(i) The development of reporting by penal institutions and the Probation and After-Care Service covering receptions, occurrences during treatment, and discharges, with provision for linking these reports with the relevant police reports within a computer (paragraphs 37(c), 48(f) and 103).

(j) The use of a single computer organization for criminal and penal statistics, including records of offences, court proceedings and penal treatments, to serve all users of the statistics (paragraphs 94, 103 and 104).

(k) The revision of the published statistics to incorporate the following:

(i) The earliest practicable presentation after the end of each year of sufficient statistical material, in advance of the remainder of the statistics, to indicate the main trends in crime and criminal proceedings during the year (paragraphs 111(a) and 113 to 118).

(ii) The separation of the remaining contents of the statistics into different parts designed to serve different users. Two parts would provide comprehensive national statistics about offences and offenders in the degree of detail required by specialist users. A further part would provide regional statistics, and another would be devoted to motoring offences. The final part would be a digest of more general interest, providing guidance in the interpretation of the statistics and varying in content from year to year. This separation would also enable some material to be published earlier in the year than would be possible if the statistics were published in one volume (paragraph 111).

(iii) The addition of new tables analysing offences according to the circumstances in which they occur and to the characteristics of offenders, and relating these factors to sentencing and to the outcome of treatment in terms of reconviction (paragraphs 111 and 121).

(iv) The inclusion in each volume of an authoritative commentary written by a professional statistician possessed of the necessary background knowledge of criminal law, police practice and the penal system (paragraphs 127 and 130).

The first five parts of the proposed Criminal Statistics would replace the present

Appendix C   145

Criminal Statistics, the Supplementary Statistics and the Annual Return of Offences Relating to Motor Vehicles, and would provide scope for eliminating some of the statistical material at present included in the annual Report on the work of the Prison Department.

Appendix D
Specimen Pages from Tables I(a), II(a) and V of the *Criminal Statistics,* 1968

These pages from the *Criminal Statistics* are included to enable the reader who does not have a copy at hand to study the layout of three of the tables concerned with sentencing. They are extracts only, and not reproductions of the complete tables, which cover several pages; nor do they include the explanatory footnotes.

The extract from Table I(*a*) shows the difference between judicial statistics for offences (such as malicious woundings) which are often dealt with summarily by the magistrates' courts and those (such as more serious violence) which are usually or always committed to higher courts for trial (for which columns (10) to (33) are therefore blank). The results of these trial by higher courts can be studied in Table II(*a*). The results of appeals against conviction or sentence by higher courts can be seen from Table V.

The offences, or groups of offences, are numbered according to the Home Office's classification system, which is set out in Appendix IV of the *Criminal Statistics*. Thus – to take the first composite group, 16–18 – offence 16 is buggery, offence 17 is attempts thereat, and offence 18 is indecency between males.

TABLE I (a)—
Persons proceeded against (all ages).

OFFENCE		Number apprehended	Number summoned	Total number proceeded against	Discharged under s. 7, Magistrate Courts Act, 1952	Detained	Bailed	Charge withdrawn or dismissed	Hospital or Guardianship order (No finding of guilt)	Total found guilty	Absolute Discharge	Recognizances	Conditional Discharge
(1)		(2)	(3)	(4)	(5)	(6)	(7)	(8)	(9)	(10)	(11)	(12)	(13)
Section (A)—INDICTABLE OFFENCES													
CLASS I—OFFENCES AGAINST THE PERSON													
1 Murder: 1 Of persons aged 1 year or over	M	225	—	225	2	219	4	—	—	—	—	—	—
	F	32	—	32	1	24	7	—	—	—	—	—	—
2 Of infants under 1 year of age	M	9	—	9	1	6	2	—	—	—	—	—	—
	F	6	—	6	1	3	2	—	—	—	—	—	—
2 Attempted murder	M	197	2	199	—	155	40	2	—	—	—	—	—
	F	24	—	24	4	6	8	6	—	—	—	—	—
3 Threats, conspiracy or incitement to murder	M	41	3	44	—	24	17	—	—	3	—	—	1
	F	4	—	4	—	—	4	—	—	—	—	—	—
4 Manslaughter	M	58	4	62	2	19	41	—	—	—	—	—	—
	F	22	1	23	2	6	15	—	—	—	—	—	—
4A Infanticide	F	20	2	22	—	9	13	—	—	—	—	—	—
4B Child destruction	M	—	—	—	—	—	—	—	—	—	—	—	—
	F	—	—	—	—	—	—	—	—	—	—	—	—
4C Causing death by dangerous driving	M	55	434	489	12	13	458	5	—	1	—	—	1
	F	1	27	28	2	—	25	1	—	—	—	—	—
5 Wounding	M	1,496	73	1,569	50	473	937	51	—	43	—	—	5
	F	64	6	70	2	8	50	5	—	5	—	—	—
6 Endangering railway passengers	M	19	22	41	—	1	19	1	—	20	—	—	4
	F	—	—	—	—	—	—	—	—	—	—	—	—
7 Endangering life at sea	M	—	—	—	—	—	—	—	—	—	—	—	—
	F	—	—	—	—	—	—	—	—	—	—	—	—
8 Malicious wounding	M	10,556	7,230	17,786	55	218	1,229	2,205	6	13,827	187	314	1,453
	F	574	475	1,049	3	6	48	194	1	773	20	60	195
9 Assault	M	103	141	244	—	7	11	32	—	182	3	5	18
	F	7	10	17	1	—	—	1	—	13	—	2	3
10 Intimidation and molestation	M	—	—	—	—	—	—	—	—	—	—	—	—
	F	—	—	—	—	—	—	—	—	—	—	—	—
11 Cruelty to children	M	—	—	—	—	—	—	—	—	—	—	—	—
	F	—	—	—	—	—	—	—	—	—	—	—	—
12 Abandoning children under 2 years of age	M	1	—	1	—	—	—	1	—	—	—	—	—
	F	6	—	6	—	—	1	1	—	4	—	—	1
13 Child stealing	M	12	1	13	3	4	5	1	—	—	—	—	—
	F	8	—	8	—	3	3	—	—	2	—	—	—
14 Procuring abortion	M	33	3	36	1	4	30	1	—	—	—	—	—
	F	27	12	39	—	1	38	—	—	—	—	—	—
15 Concealment of birth	M	—	—	—	—	—	—	—	—	—	—	—	—
	F	3	2	5	—	—	—	—	—	5	1	—	1

MAGISTRATES' COURTS
Nature of offences and results of proceedings

Hospital Order under s. 60, Mental Health Act, 1959 (14)	Probation Order (15)	Fit Person Order (16)	Fine (17)	Attendance Centre (18)	Detention Centre (19)	Approved School (20)	Police Cells (21)	Suspended Sentence (22)	Imprisonment (immediate) without option of fine — Total (23)	14 days and under (24)	Over 14 days and up to 1 month (25)	Over 1 month and up to 2 months (26)	Over 2 months and up to 3 months (27)	Over 3 months and up to 6 months (28)	Over 6 months (29)	Committed for sentence under s. 29, Magistrates' Courts Act, 1952 (30)	Committed for sentence under s. 28, Magistrates' Courts Act, 1952 (31)	Otherwise dealt with (32)	Proceedings not completed (33)
—	—	—	—	—	—	—	—	—	—	—	—	—	—	—	—	—	—	—	—
—	—	—	—	—	—	—	—	—	—	—	—	—	—	—	—	—	—	—	—
—	—	—	—	—	—	—	—	—	—	—	—	—	—	—	—	—	—	—	1
—	2	—	—	—	—	—	—	—	—	—	—	—	—	—	—	—	—	—	—
—	—	—	—	—	—	—	—	—	—	—	—	—	—	—	—	—	—	—	—
—	—	—	—	—	—	—	—	—	—	—	—	—	—	—	—	—	—	—	—
—	—	—	—	—	—	—	—	—	—	—	—	—	—	—	—	—	—	—	—
—	—	—	—	—	—	—	—	—	—	—	—	—	—	—	—	—	—	—	—
1	12/2	—	12	—	5	3/3	—	—	—	—	—	—	—	—	—	—	5	—	15
—	1	1	14	—	—	—	—	—	—	—	—	—	—	—	—	—	—	—	—
—	—	—	—	—	—	—	—	—	—	—	—	—	—	—	—	—	—	—	—
57/6	677/117	7/1	8,513/305	125	309/5	44/6	3	985/36	779/11	4	37/3	42	278/4	418/4	—	247/8	84/3	43	246/24
3	17/4	—	111/4	2	5	—	—	8	6	—	1	1	—	3	—	2	1	1	12/2
—	—	—	—	—	—	—	—	—	—	—	—	—	—	—	—	—	—	—	—
—	—	—	—	—	—	—	—	—	—	—	—	—	—	—	—	—	—	—	—
—	2	—	—	—	—	—	—	—	—	—	—	—	—	—	—	—	—	1	—
1	—	1	—	—	—	—	—	—	—	—	—	—	—	—	—	—	—	—	—
—	—	—	—	—	—	—	—	—	—	—	—	—	—	—	—	—	—	—	—
—	1	—	2	—	—	—	—	—	—	—	—	—	—	—	—	—	—	—	—

TABLE II(a)—ASSIZES
Persons for trial (all ages).

OFFENCE		Total number for trial	No prosecution	Unfit to plead	Acquitted	Not guilty by reason of insanity	Total found guilty	Absolute Discharge	Recognizances
			NOT TRIED						
(1)		(2)	(3)	(4)	(5)	(6)	(7)	(8)	(9)
CLASS I—OFFENCES AGAINST THE PERSON									
1 Murder	M	90	—	2	15	—	73	—	—
	F	10	—	1	7	1	1	—	—
2 Attempted murder	M	58	—	3	12	—	43	1	1
	F	5	—	—	1	1	3	—	—
3 Threats, conspiracy or incitement to murder	M	31	—	—	2	—	29	—	4
	F	3	—	—	—	—	3	—	1
4 Manslaughter:									
Manslaughter under s. 2, Homicide Act, 1957	M	33	—	—	—	—	33	—	—
	F	11	—	—	—	—	11	—	—
Other manslaughter	M	119	—	—	17	—	102	2	2
	F	22	—	—	5	1	16	—	—
4A Infanticide	M	—	—	—	—	—	—	—	—
	F	24	—	—	—	—	24	—	—
4B Child destruction	M	—	—	—	—	—	—	—	—
	F	—	—	—	—	—	—	—	—
4C Causing death by dangerous driving	M	484	—	—	130	—	354	—	—
	F	22	—	—	8	—	14	1	—
5 Wounding	M	884	3	3	215	—	663	—	4
	F	51	—	—	12	—	39	—	1
6 Endangering railway passengers	M	16	—	—	—	—	16	—	4
	F	—	—	—	—	—	—	—	—
7 Endangering life at sea	M	1	—	—	1	—	—	—	—
	F	—	—	—	—	—	—	—	—
8 Malicious wounding	M	2,142	12	5	424	—	1,701	7	23
	F	84	1	—	20	—	63	2	4
9 Assault	M	176	—	—	5	—	171	2	7
	F	7	—	—	1	—	6	—	—
10 Intimidation and molestation	M	—	—	—	—	—	—	—	—
	F	—	—	—	—	—	—	—	—
11 Cruelty to children	M	10	—	—	1	—	9	—	—
	F	16	1	—	4	—	11	—	—
12 Abandoning children under 2 years of age	M	1	—	—	—	—	1	—	—
	F	—	—	—	—	—	—	—	—
13 Child stealing	M	14	1	—	2	—	11	—	—
	F	4	—	—	1	—	3	—	—
14 Procuring abortion	M	27	1	—	5	—	21	1	—
	F	41	—	—	2	—	39	—	2
15 Concealment of birth	M	—	—	—	—	—	—	—	—
	F	—	—	—	—	—	—	—	—
16 Buggery	M	205	1	1	9	—	194	—	1
	F	2	—	—	—	—	2	—	—
17 Attempt to commit buggery, &c.	M	187	1	—	33	—	153	—	—
	F	1	—	—	1	—	—	—	—

AND QUARTER SESSIONS
Nature of offences and results of proceedings

FOUND GUILTY AND SENTENCED, &C.

Conditional Discharge (10)	Hospital Order under s. 60, Mental Health Act, 1959 (11)	Restriction Order under s. 65, Mental Health Act, 1959 (12)	Probation Order (13)	Fine (14)	Detention Centre (15)	Approved School (16)	Borstal Training (17)	Returned to Borstal (18)	Suspended Sentence (19)	Imprisonment (Immediate) (20)	Extended Sentence (21)	Otherwise disposed of (22)
—	—	—	—	—	—	—	—	—	—	67	—	6
—	1	9	8	—	—	—	1	—	1	1	—	1
2	—	1	3	—	—	—	—	—	—	20	—	—
1	—	—	8	—	—	1	—	—	10	4	—	—
1	5	18	—	—	—	—	—	—	—	9	—	—
—	1	4	4	—	—	—	—	—	—	1	—	1
3	—	6	3	—	—	—	3	—	9	73	—	1
1	—	2	4	—	—	—	—	—	3	6	—	—
—	2	—	21	—	—	—	—	—	—	1	—	—
6	—	—	4	282	3	—	4	—	22	32	—	1
—	—	—	—	12	—	—	—	—	—	—	—	1
14	9	27	38	20	26	1	66	—	77	380	—	1
1	—	2	15	—	—	—	1	—	2	18	—	—
—	—	—	1	1	—	—	—	—	6	3	—	—
85	7	9	131	279	97	2	103	7	332	616	—	3
6	1	3	18	4	1	—	1	—	19	4	—	—
21	—	1	14	62	6	—	3	1	25	29	—	—
—	—	—	1	—	—	—	—	—	1	4	—	—
—	—	—	1	1	—	—	—	—	2	5	—	—
—	2	—	4	—	—	—	—	—	—	5	—	—
—	1	1	1	—	—	—	—	—	1	4	—	—
—	1	—	1	1	—	—	—	—	—	1	—	—
1	—	—	1	1	—	—	—	—	8	9	—	—
3	—	—	4	—	—	—	—	—	15	15	—	—
10	1	11	33	6	—	—	5	—	33	94	—	—
—	—	—	—	—	—	—	—	—	2	—	—	—
7	1	2	36	18	—	—	2	—	20	66	1	—

TABLE V—COURT OF APPEAL (CRIMINAL DIVISION)

Offences of which appellants were convicted, and number and results of the appeals

(1) OFFENCE	(2) Total	APPLICATIONS FOR LEAVE TO APPEAL							APPEALS HEARD OR OTHERWISE DISPOSED OF											
		(3) Against conviction	(4) Against sentence	(5) Against conviction and sentence	(6) Abandoned	(7) Refused	(8) Granted	(9) Total	(10) After leave granted	(11) On grounds involving questions of law	(12) With certificate of Judge at trial	(13) Abandoned	(14) Conviction affirmed	(15) Conviction quashed, conviction of some other offence substituted	(16) Conviction quashed	(17) Sentence affirmed	(18) Sentence quashed, some other sentence substituted	(19) Sentence quashed	(20) Retrial
CLASS I: OFFENCES AGAINST THE PERSON																			
1 Murder	40	40	—	—	3	29	8	8	8	—	—	—	4	4	—	—	—	—	—
2 Attempts to murder	11	—	7	4	6	5	—	—	—	—	—	—	—	—	—	—	1	—	—
3 Threats or conspiracy to murder	3	—	3	—	2	—	1	1	1	—	—	—	—	—	—	—	—	—	—
4 Manslaughter	54	10	30	14	18	26	10	10	10	—	—	—	3	—	—	1	5	1	—
4(c) Causing death by dangerous driving	20	2	12	6	6	10	4	4	4	—	—	—	—	—	1	1	1	1	—
5 Felonious wounding	177	22	103	52	61	92	24	27	24	2	1	—	10	—	1	6	9	1	—
6 Endangering railway passengers	3	—	—	—	2	1	—	—	—	—	—	—	—	—	—	—	—	—	—
8 Malicious wounding	336	53	182	101	220	84	32	32	32	—	—	—	14	1	2	5	9	1	—
9 Assault	7	—	5	2	3	4	—	—	—	—	—	—	—	—	5	—	—	—	—
11 Cruelty to children	2	—	1	1	2	—	—	—	—	—	—	—	—	—	—	—	—	—	—
14 Abortion	12	1	11	—	6	4	2	2	2	—	—	—	—	—	—	—	1	—	—
15 Concealment of birth	2	—	2	—	—	—	2	2	2	—	—	—	—	—	—	—	—	—	—
16–18 Buggery, &c.	80	6	60	14	41	28	11	11	11	—	—	1	1	—	—	1	2	—	—
19 Rape	71	10	43	18	36	27	8	8	8	—	—	—	1	—	2	3	6	—	—
20–22 Indecent assault, &c., on females	95	6	74	15	56	27	12	12	12	—	—	—	—	—	1	3	7	1	1
23 Incest	21	1	16	4	17	3	1	1	1	—	—	—	—	—	—	—	1	—	—
24 Procuration	26	6	9	11	14	10	2	2	2	—	—	—	—	—	2	—	—	—	—
25 Abduction	4	—	3	1	—	1	3	3	3	—	—	—	—	—	—	—	3	—	—
26 Bigamy	8	—	7	1	6	1	1	1	1	—	—	—	—	—	1	—	—	—	—
74 Gross indecency with children (Indecency with children Act, 1960)	4	1	3	—	2	—	2	2	2	—	—	—	—	—	—	—	1	—	—
Total of Class I	976	158	573	245	501	352	123	126	123	2	1	1	33	5	15	20	46	5	1

Table of indictable offences (columns unlabelled on this page)

CLASS II: OFFENCES AGAINST PROPERTY WITH VIOLENCE																				
27–33 Breaking and entering	1,368	112	1,083	173	982	271	119	115	115	3	1	1	12	–	–	10	20	72	4	1
34 Robbery	499	68	317	114	280	190	30	29	29	1	–	1	5	2	–	2	12	7	1	–
35 Blackmail	31	7	14	10	19	10	2	2	2	–	–	–	1	–	–	2	–	1	–	–
Total of Class II	1,898	187	1,414	297	1,281	471	151	146	146	4	1	1	18	2	2	12	32	80	5	1
CLASS III: OFFENCES AGAINST PROPERTY WITHOUT VIOLENCE																				
37 Embezzlement	15	1	9	5	11	2	2	2	2	–	–	–	1	–	–	1	1	–	–	–
38–49 Larceny	752	88	516	148	515	163	77	74	74	2	1	–	13	–	–	12	14	32	4	2
50–53 Frauds and false pretences	195	42	109	44	97	69	31	29	29	2	1	–	8	–	–	7	5	7	3	1
54 Receiving stolen goods	357	70	196	91	188	121	53	48	48	3	2	–	14	–	–	11	2	22	3	1
55 Offences in bankruptcy	6	1	5	–	3	2	2	1	1	1	–	–	1	–	–	–	–	–	1	–
Total of Class III	1,325	202	835	288	814	357	165	154	154	8	3	–	36	–	–	31	22	61	11	4
CLASS IV: MALICIOUS INJURIES TO PROPERTY																				
56 Arson	38	2	33	3	20	15	3	3	3	–	–	–	–	–	–	–	–	3	–	–
57 Other malicious injuries to property	16	1	9	6	13	2	1	1	1	–	–	–	–	–	–	1	–	–	–	–
Total of Class IV	54	3	42	9	33	17	4	4	4	–	–	–	–	–	1	–	3	3	–	1
CLASS V: FORGERY AND OFFENCES AGAINST THE CURRENCY																				
58–59 Forgery	56	7	40	9	37	17	2	2	2	–	–	–	–	–	–	–	1	2	–	–
Total of Class V	56	7	40	9	37	17	2	2	2	–	–	–	–	–	–	–	1	2	–	–
CLASS VI: OTHER OFFENCES NOT INCLUDED IN THE ABOVE CLASSES																				
63–66 Offences against the State and Public Order	37	3	16	18	12	18	7	7	7	–	–	–	–	–	–	–	6	1	–	–
67 Perjury	15	2	12	1	12	3	–	–	–	–	–	–	–	–	–	–	–	–	–	1
70–72 Motoring offences	123	23	65	35	50	57	16	16	16	–	–	–	2	–	3	6	6	4	–	–
99 Other indictable offences	132	21	62	49	63	50	22	19	19	1	–	–	4	–	5	3	3	7	3	1
Total of Class VI	307	49	155	103	137	128	45	42	42	1	2	–	6	–	7	8	15	12	3	1
TOTAL OF INDICTABLE OFFENCES	4,616	606	3,059	951	2,803	1,342	471	493	471	15	7	2	93	2	7	66	90	204	24	7

References

For the main sources of English criminal statistics see Appendix B.

Ackman, D. A., Figlio, R., and Normandeau, A. (1967), 'Concerning the measurement of delinquency: a rejoinder and beyond', *British Journal of Criminology*, vol. 7, pp. 442–9.

Andenaes, J. (1966), 'The general preventive effects of punishment,' *University of Pennsylvania Law Review*, vol. 114, no. 7, pp. 949 ff.

Andry, R. G. (1960), *Delinquency and Parental Pathology*, Methuen.

Association of Chief Police Officers of England and Wales (1966), 'Trial by jury', *New Law Journal*, vol. 116, pp. 928–31.

Belson, W. A., Millerson, G. L., and Didcott, P. J. (1968), *The Development of a Procedure for Eliciting Information from Boys about the Nature and Extent of their Stealing*, Survey Research Centre, London School of Economics.

Benson, G. (1959), 'Prediction methods and young prisoners', *British Journal of Delinquency*, vol. 9, pp. 192–9.

Beutel, F. K. (1957), *Some Potentialities of Experimental Jurisprudence as a New Branch of Social Science*, University of Nebraska Press.

Carr-Hill, R. A. (1970), 'Victims of our typologies', *The Violent Offender – Reality or Illusion?*, Blackwell.

Christiansen, K. O. (ed.) (1965), *Scandinavian Studies in Criminology*, vol. 1, Tavistock.

Committee on Homosexual Offences and Prostitution (1957), *Report of the Committee on Homosexual Offences and Prostitution* (Chairman: Sir John Wolfenden) Cmnd. 247, HMSO.

Conway, F. (1967), *Sampling: An Introduction for Social Scientists*, Allen & Unwin.

Departmental Committee on Criminal Statistics (1967), *Report of the Departmental Committee on Criminal Statistics* (Chairman: Mr W. Perks), HMSO, Cmnd. 3448.

Departmental Committee on Jury Service (1965), *Report of the Departmental Committee on Jury Service* (Chairman: Lord Morris), HMSO, Cmnd. 2627.

Departmental Committee on the Probation Service (1962), *First Report of the Departmental Committee on the Probation Service* (Chairman: Mr R. P. Morison), HMSO.

Douglas, J. W. B., Ross, J. M., Hammond, W. H., and Mulligan, D. G. (1967), 'Delinquency and social class', *British Journal of Criminology*, vol. 7, no. 2, pp. 294 ff.

Ennis, P. H. (1967), *Criminal Victimization in the United States: A Report of a National Survey*, US Government Printing Office, Washington, DC.

Glueck, S., and Glueck, E. (1950), *Unravelling Juvenile Delinquency*, Harper & Row.

Grant, J. D., and Grant, M. Q. (1959), 'A group dynamics approach to the treatment of nonconformists in the Navy', *Annals of the American Academy of Political and Social Science*, vol. 322, pp. 126–35.

Grygier, T. (1966), 'The effect of social action: current prediction methods and two new models', *British Journal of Criminology*, vol. 6, pp. 269–93.

Hammond, W. H. (1960): see 'Scottish Advisory Council on the Treatment of Offenders'.

Hammond, W. H. (1969): see 'Home Office, (1969)'.

Hammond, W. H., and Chayen, E. (1963), *Persistent Criminals*, HMSO.

Home Office (1964, with later amendments), *Instructions for the Preparation of Statistics Relating to Crime*.

Home Office (1969), *The Sentence of the Court*, HMSO.

Hooton, E. (1939), *The American Criminal: An Anthropological Study* (2 vols.) Harvard University Press.

Kalven, H., and Zeisel, H. (1966), *The American Jury*, Little, Brown.

McClintock, F. H., Avison, N. H., Savill, N. C., and Worthington, V. L. (1963), *Crimes of Violence*, Macmillan.

McClintock, F. H., and Avison, N. H. (1968), *Crime in England and Wales*, Heinemann.

McCord, W., and McCord, J. (1959), *Origins of Crime: A New Evaluation of the Cambridge–Somerville Youth Study*, Columbia University Press.

McDonald, L. (1969), *Delinquency and Social Class*, Faber.

Mannheim, H., and Wilkins, L. T. (1955), *Prediction Methods in Relation to Borstal Training*, HMSO.

Martin, J. P. (1962), *Offenders as Employees*, Macmillan.

Meehl, P. E. (1954), *Clinical versus Statistical Prediction: A Theoretical Analysis and a Review of the Evidence*, University of Minnesota Press.

Oppenheim, A. N. (1966), *Questionnaire Design and Attitude Measurement*, Heinemann.

Parole Board (1970), *Annual Report, 1969*, HMSO.

Rose, G. (1966), 'Concerning the measurement of delinquency', *British Journal of Criminology*, vol. 6, pp. 414–21.

Rose, G. (1968), 'Artificial delinquent generations', *Journal of Criminal Law Criminology and Police Science*, vol. 59, no. 3, pp. 370 ff.
Royal Commission on Capital Punishment (1953), *Report of the Royal Commission on Capital Punishment, 1949–53*, HMSO.

Schwartz, R. D., and Orleans, S. (1967), 'On legal sanctions', *University of Chicago Law Review*, vol. 34, pp. 274 ff.
Scottish Advisory Council on the Treatment of Offenders (1960), *Report on the Use of Short Sentences of Imprisonment by the Courts*, HMSO.
Sellin, T., and Wolfgang, M. E. (1963), *Constructing an Index of Delinquency: A Manual*, Center of Criminological Research, University of Pennsylvania.
Sellin, T., and Wolfgang, M. E. (1964), *The Measurement of Delinquency*, Wiley.
Short, J. F., and Nye, F. I. (1957), 'Reported behavior as a criterion of deviant behavior', *Social Problems*, vol. 5, pp. 207 ff.
Simon, R. (1967), *The Jury and the Defense of Insanity*, Little, Brown.
Steer, D. J. (1971), *Police Cautions*, Blackwell.

Tornudd, P. (1968), 'The preventive effect of fines for drunkenness – a controlled experiment', in N. Christie (ed.), *Scandinavian Studies in Criminology*, vol. 2, Tavistock.
Trolle, J. (1945), *Syv Maaneder Uden Politi*, cited by Andenaes.

Uniform Crimes Report for the United States (annually), US Government Printing Office, Washington, DC.

Walker, N. (1965), *Crime and Punishment in Britain*, Edinburgh University Press, 2nd edn, revised 1970.
Walker, N. (1968), *Crime and Insanity in England*, Edinburgh University Press.
Walker, N. (1969), *Sentencing in a Rational Society*, Allen Lane The Penguin Press.
Wilkins, L. T. (1958), 'A small comparative study of the results of probation', *British Journal of Delinquency*, vol. 8.
Wilkins, L. T. (1960), *Delinquent Generations: A Home Office Research Unit Report*, HMSO.
Wilkins, L. T. (1964), *Social Deviance*, Tavistock; reprinted as *Social Policy, Action and Research*, Tavistock, 1967.
Willcock, H. D., and Stokes, J. (1968), *Deterrents and Incentives to Crime among Youths aged 15–21 Years*, Government Social Survey.
Willett, T. C (1964), *Criminal on the Road*, Tavistock.
Willmer, M. A. P. (1970), *Crime and Information Theory*, Edinburgh University Press.

156   References

Index